40+
BUSINESS
MODELS &
EXAMPLES

By

Dr. Javnyuy Joybert

By Dr. Javnyuy Joybert

40+ BUSINESS MODELS & EXAMPLES:

Practical Ways Different Businesses Make Money

By

Dr. Javnyuy Joybert

TABLE OF CONTENTS

<u>INTRODUCTION</u>

*M*any times I have seen people struggle to really start businesses even popular familiar businesses that they can observe others do it and just replicate and improve. I decided to curate and put together these business models with clear examples of how these businesses make money and the actionable tips you can take to implement these businesses in your area.

I used the word agency a lot because I want to intentionally push people who go through this book to move beyond setting up self-employed businesses but agencies where they can recruit employees and or people they can pay on commission.

As you go through this book the following will happen to you;

- You will see a business model you can replicate and start making money

- You will see a business model you can improve and implement

- You will see a business model you can merge with another model and implement

- You will be inspired to generate a total new business model because the different ideas in the book will spark your creativity.

This book will transform you forever. Dig deep. Get a pen and a journal and see your life change.

CHAPTER 1:

RESTAURANT'S BUSINESS MODEL

A restaurant's primary source of revenue is the sale of food and drinks to customers. However, there are several ways a restaurant can increase its profits and make the most of its resources.

Here are some practical business models that restaurants can use to make money:

Offer takeout and delivery services: Many people prefer to order food from the comfort of their own home, and providing takeout and delivery services can increase a restaurant's customer base and sales.

Use social media and online platforms to promote the business: A strong online presence can help a restaurant attract new customers and promote special offers and events.

Host events: Restaurants can host events such as private parties, cooking classes, or live music nights to bring in additional revenue.

Offer catering services: Catering events such as weddings, corporate events, or private parties can be a lucrative business for a restaurant.

Partner with local businesses: Partnering with local businesses such as hotels or event venues can bring in a steady stream of customers.

Optimize menu pricing: Carefully considering the cost of ingredients and desired profit margin can help a restaurant set menu prices that are fair for both the business and the customer.

Offer loyalty programs: Loyalty programs can help a restaurant retain its regular customers and encourage them to visit more often.

In conclusion, there are many ways that a restaurant can make money beyond just selling food and drinks to customers. By offering a range of services and staying up-to-date with current trends and customer preferences, a restaurant can increase its profits and build a successful business.

CHAPTER 2:

SECONDARY SCHOOL BUSINESS MODEL

Secondary schools in Africa can use several business models to generate revenue and sustain their operations.

Here are some practical ways that a secondary school can make money:

Tuition fees: Charging tuition fees is the primary source of revenue for most secondary schools in Africa.

Grants and donations: Schools can apply for grants from government agencies, foundations, and other organizations to fund specific projects or cover operating costs. Schools can also solicit donations from individuals and businesses to support their programs.

Partnerships and sponsorships: Schools can partner with local businesses or organizations to provide resources or funding in exchange for promotional opportunities. Schools can also seek sponsorships from companies to support specific events or initiatives.

Renting out facilities: Schools can rent out their facilities for events such as weddings, conferences, or sports tournaments to generate additional revenue.

Offering additional services: Schools can offer additional services such as after-school programs, tutoring, or summer camps to generate additional revenue.

<u>Selling school merchandise:</u> Schools can sell branded merchandise such as t-shirts, hats, or other items to students, parents, and alumni to raise funds.

In conclusion, there are several ways that a secondary school in Africa can generate revenue and sustain its operations. By diversifying its sources of funding and offering a range of services, a school can create a strong and sustainable business model.

CHAPTER 3:

PRIVATE UNIVERSITY BUSINESS MODEL

*P*rivate universities in Africa rely on a variety of business models to generate revenue and sustain their operations.

Here are some practical ways that a private university can make money:

Tuition fees: Charging tuition fees is the primary source of revenue for most private universities in Africa.

Grants and donations: Universities can apply for grants from government agencies, foundations, and other organizations to fund specific projects or cover operating costs. Universities can also solicit

7

donations from individuals and businesses to support their programs.

Partnerships and sponsorships: Universities can partner with local businesses or organizations to provide resources or funding in exchange for promotional opportunities. Universities can also seek sponsorships from companies to support specific events or initiatives.

Renting out facilities: Universities can rent out their facilities for events such as conferences, sports tournaments, or concerts to generate additional revenue.

Offering additional services: Universities can offer additional services such as continuing education courses, executive education programs, short certification programs or consulting services to generate additional revenue.

Selling university merchandise: Universities can sell branded merchandise such as t-shirts, hats, or other items to students, alumni, and the general public to raise funds.

In conclusion, private universities in Africa can use a variety of business models to generate revenue and sustain their operations. By diversifying their sources of funding and offering a range of services, private universities can create a strong and sustainable business model.

CHAPTER 3:

HEALTH CLINIC BUSINESS MODEL

*H*ealth clinics in Africa can use several business models to generate revenue and sustain their operations. Here are some practical ways that a health clinic can make money:

Charging for medical services: The most common way that health clinics make money is by charging for medical services such as consultations, treatments, and procedures.

Charging for medical services is a common business model for health clinics in Africa and around the world. When patients visit a health clinic, they typically pay a fee for the medical services they receive, such as consultations with a doctor or nurse, diagnostic tests, and treatments or procedures. These fees can vary based on the type of service provided, the duration of the service, and the expertise of the healthcare provider.

Accepting insurance: Many health clinics in Africa accept insurance from private companies or government programs to cover the cost of medical services.

Health clinics that accept insurance typically enter into agreements with insurance companies to become "in-network" providers. This means that the clinic agrees to accept the insurance company's approved payment rate for the medical services it provides. Patients who visit in-network health clinics typically pay lower co-payments or deductibles than they would at out-of-network clinics.

By accepting insurance, health clinics are able to increase their patient base and generate additional revenue. However, the clinic must follow the insurance company's guidelines and billing procedures, which can be time-consuming and complex. It is important for health clinics to carefully consider the benefits and challenges of accepting insurance before entering into agreements with insurance companies.

Grants and donations: Health clinics can apply for grants from government agencies, foundations, and other organizations to fund specific projects or cover operating costs. Health clinics can also solicit donations from individuals and businesses to support their programs.

Partnerships and sponsorships: Health clinics can partner with local businesses or organizations to provide resources or funding in exchange for promotional opportunities or affordable health care services to their staff body. Health clinics can also seek sponsorships from companies to support specific events or initiatives.

Renting out facilities: Health clinics can rent out their facilities for events such as conferences or training sessions to generate additional revenue.

Offering additional services: Health clinics can offer additional services such as wellness programs, nutrition counseling, or physical therapy to generate additional revenue.

Here is an example of how offering additional services can work for a health clinic:

A primary care clinic in a small town in Africa wants to generate additional revenue and expand its services to patients. The clinic decides to offer a wellness program that includes group exercise classes, nutrition counseling, and stress management workshops.

To promote the wellness program, the clinic creates flyers and social media posts advertising the program and its benefits. The clinic also reaches out to local businesses and organizations to promote the program and offer discounted rates for employees or members who sign up.

The wellness program proves to be popular, and the clinic is able to attract new patients who are interested in improving their overall health and wellness. The clinic charges a fee for participation in the program, which generates additional revenue for the clinic.

In addition to attracting new patients and generating additional revenue, the wellness program also helps to improve the health and well-being of the clinic's patients, which can lead to long-term cost savings for both the patients and the clinic.

In conclusion, there are several ways that a health clinic in Africa can generate revenue and sustain its operations. By diversifying its sources of funding and offering a range of services, a health clinic can create a strong and sustainable business model.

CHAPTER 4:

EVENTS PLANNING AND EXECUTION AGENCY BUSINESS MODEL

*E*vents planning and execution agencies in Africa can use several business models to generate revenue and sustain their operations.

Here are some practical ways that an events planning and execution agency can make money:

<u>**Charging for event planning and execution**</u> <u>**services:**</u> The most common way that events planning and execution agencies make money is by charging for their services, which can include planning and organizing events, coordinating

vendors and suppliers, and managing event itself and logistics.

Commission-based fees: Some events planning and execution agencies may charge a commission on top of their fees, based on the total cost of the event they are planning.

Commission-based fees are a business model used by some events planning and execution agencies in Africa and around the world. Under this model, the agency charges a percentage of the total cost of the event as a fee for its services. For example, if the agency charges a 15% commission on the total cost of the event, and the total cost of the event is $50,000, the agency's fee would be $7,500.

This business model can be beneficial for events planning and execution agencies, as it allows them to earn additional revenue based on the size and complexity of the events they are planning. It can also be attractive to clients, as it aligns the interests of the agency with those of the client, as the agency's fee increases as the total cost of the event increases.

Here is an example of how commission-based fees can work for an events planning and execution agency:

A corporate events planning and execution agency is hired to plan a company's annual conference, which is expected to cost $100,000. The agency charges a 20% commission on the total cost of the event, which means that its fee will be $20,000.

The agency works closely with the company to plan and execute the conference, coordinating vendors, managing logistics, and promoting the event. The conference is a success, and the agency earns a fee of $20,000 for its services.

In this example, the events planning and execution agency is able to earn additional revenue based on the size and complexity of the conference it planned. The commission-based fee model aligns the interests of the agency with those of the client, as the agency's fee increases as the total cost of the event increases.

Renting out event equipment and supplies:

Agencies can rent out event equipment and supplies such as tables, chairs, linens, and audio-visual equipment(cameras, speakers etc) to generate additional revenue.

Offering event marketing and promotion services:

Agencies can offer marketing and promotion services to event clients, such as creating social media campaigns or developing marketing materials, sale event tickets for clients on commission to generate additional revenue.

Partnerships and sponsorships: Agencies can partner with local businesses or organizations to provide resources or funding in exchange for promotional opportunities. Agencies can also seek sponsorships from companies to support specific events or initiatives. The agency can also sign a working agreement with local businesses and organizations to be their primary event planner and organizer for both internal and external event

Selling event merchandise: Agencies can sell branded merchandise such as t-shirts, hats, or other items at events to raise funds.

In conclusion, there are several ways that an events planning and execution agency in Africa can generate revenue and sustain its operations. By diversifying its sources of funding and offering a range of services, an agency can create a strong and sustainable business model.

Note: Merging Restuarant and Events planning agency business model can lead to an incredible business.

CHAPTER 5:

LAUNDRY SERVICE BUSINESS MODEL

Laundry service businesses in Africa can make money in several ways, including:

Charging customers for washing, drying, and folding their laundry: This is the most common way for laundry businesses to make money, as customers are willing to pay for the convenience of having someone else take care of their laundry.

Offering pickup and delivery services: Some laundry businesses in Africa offer pickup and delivery services for an additional fee, allowing customers to have their laundry picked up from their homes or offices and delivered back to them once it has been cleaned and pressed.

Providing dry cleaning services: Many laundry businesses in Africa also offer dry cleaning services for items that cannot be washed in water, such as suits and dresses. These services typically come with a higher price tag, as they require specialized equipment and chemicals.

Selling laundry-related products: Laundry businesses can also make money by selling laundry-related products, such as detergent, fabric softener, and dryer sheets. This can be a good way to generate additional revenue and keep customers coming back to the store.

As a young entrepreneur looking to start a laundry business in Africa, it is important to focus on providing high-quality services and building a strong customer base. Some tips for success include:

Invest in good equipment and supplies, such as washing machines and dryers, to ensure that you can provide fast and efficient service to your customers.

Offer competitive pricing and consider offering discounts or loyalty programs to attract and retain customers.

Consider offering additional services, such as ironing or mending, to differentiate your business from competitors and increase your revenue streams.

Keep your store clean and well-maintained, and train your employees to provide excellent customer service.

Overall, the key to success in the laundry business in Africa is to provide high-quality services, build a strong customer base, and continuously look for ways to improve and expand your business.

CHAPTER 6:

NANNY AGENCY BUSINESS MODEL

A nanny agency is a business that connects families with caregivers who are responsible for the care and supervision of children. Nanny agencies typically make money by charging a fee to families for their services, which may include screening and placing caregivers, providing ongoing support and resources, and handling payroll and tax-related responsibilities for the caregivers they place.

In Africa, the practical business model for a nanny agency may involve working with both local and international families to find caregivers who meet their specific needs and preferences. This may include caregivers who are trained in early childhood education, have experience working with children with special needs, or are fluent in multiple languages.

To be successful in this industry, it is important for nanny agencies to have a strong network of qualified caregivers, as well as a thorough understanding of the local market and the needs of families.

Some actionable tips for starting a nanny agency in Africa include:

- Research the local market to understand the demand for nanny services and the competitive landscape.

- Develop a strong network of caregivers who meet the needs of families in your target market.

- Establish clear policies and procedures for screening and placing caregivers, including background checks and reference checks.

- Offer ongoing support and resources to both caregivers and families to ensure a successful placement.
- Consider offering additional services such as payroll and tax support to make your agency a one-stop shop for families.

There are several ways that a nanny agency can make money:

Placement fees: Many nanny agencies in Africa charge a fee to families for their services, which may include screening and placing caregivers, providing ongoing support and resources, and handling payroll and tax-related responsibilities for the caregivers they place.

Ongoing fees: Some nanny agencies in Africa charge ongoing fees to families for their services, such as monthly or annual fees for access to a pool of caregivers or for ongoing support and resources.

Payroll and tax services: Some nanny agencies in Africa offer payroll and tax services to caregivers, which may include calculating and paying taxes, handling payroll and benefits, and providing other related support. These services may be offered to caregivers for an additional fee.

Referral fees: Nanny agencies in Africa may charge referral fees to other agencies or organizations that refer families to their services.

Educational courses and resources: Some nanny agencies in Africa offer educational courses or resources, such as training programs or online resources, to caregivers for an additional fee.

Advertising and marketing services: Nanny agencies in Africa may also offer advertising and marketing services to families or caregivers, such as assistance with creating online profiles or advertising on their website or social media channels.

Partnerships and sponsorships: Nanny agencies in Africa may also generate revenue through partnerships or sponsorships with other companies or organizations.

The business model for a nanny agency in Africa may involve a combination of these revenue streams, depending on the specific services and offerings of the agency.

Overall, starting a nanny agency in Africa can be a rewarding and lucrative business opportunity for young entrepreneurs who are passionate about helping families and caregivers connect. With careful planning and a focus on providing high-quality services, you can build a successful nanny agency that meets the needs of families in your community.

CHAPTER 7:

SOFTWARE DEVELOPMENT AGENCY BUSINESS MODEL

A software development agency is a business that specializes in creating software solutions for clients. These solutions may include custom software applications, mobile apps, website development, and other related services.

While it is not necessary to be a software engineer in order to run a software development agency, it is important to have a strong business mindset, leadership abilities, and sales skills in order to succeed. In order to deliver high-quality software development services to clients, it is also essential to hire a team of skilled software engineers and developers who are familiar with the latest technologies and trends.

Having a forward-thinking approach and the ability to anticipate the needs of clients will also be key to the success of a software development agency.

In Africa, the practical business model for a software development agency may involve working with a variety of clients, including small and medium-sized businesses, startups, and larger organizations. The agency may offer a range of services, such as custom software development, website design and development, mobile app development, and maintenance and support services.

To be successful in this industry, it is important for a software development agency to have a strong team of experienced developers, a thorough understanding of the latest technologies and trends, and a focus on delivering high-quality solutions to clients.

Some actionable tips for starting a software development agency in Africa include:

- Research the local market to understand the demand for software development services and the competitive landscape.

- Assemble a team of experienced and skilled developers who are familiar with the latest technologies and trends.

- Offer a range of services to meet the needs of different clients, such as custom software development, website design and development, and mobile app development.

- Establish clear policies and procedures for working with clients, including project scope, timelines, and pricing.

- Focus on delivering high-quality solutions that meet the needs and expectations of clients.

Overall, starting a software development agency in Africa can be a rewarding and lucrative business opportunity for young entrepreneurs who are passionate about technology and problem-solving. With careful planning and a focus on delivering excellent services, you can build a successful software development agency that meets the needs of clients in your community.

There are several ways that a software development agency can make money in Africa:

Project-based fees: Many software development agencies in Africa charge fees for their services on a project-by-project basis. This may include an upfront fee for the development of a custom software application or website, as well as ongoing maintenance and support fees.

Hourly rates: Some software development agencies in Africa charge clients an hourly rate for their services, which may include custom software development, website design and development, and mobile app development.

Maintenance and support services: Software development agencies in Africa may also generate revenue through maintenance and support services, such as bug fixing, updates, and ongoing support for clients' software applications and websites.

Reselling products or services: Software development agencies in Africa may also generate revenue by reselling products or services, such as hosting or cloud services, to clients.

Partnerships and sponsorships: Software development agencies in Africa may also generate revenue through partnerships or sponsorships with other companies or organizations.

Overall, the business model for a software development agency in Africa may involve a combination of these revenue streams, depending on the specific services and offerings of the agency.

By Dr. Javnyuy Joybert

CHAPTER 8:

BUSINESS MODEL FOR A CORPORATE COMMUNICATION AGENCY

A corporate communication agency is a business that helps organizations communicate effectively with their stakeholders, including employees, customers, investors, and the media. This may involve developing and implementing communication strategies, creating marketing materials and campaigns, and providing public relations and media relations support.

In Africa, the practical business model for a corporate communication agency may involve working with a variety of clients, including small and medium-sized businesses, startups, and larger organizations. The agency may offer a range of services, such as brand development and management, media relations, internal communication, and crisis communication.

To be successful in this industry, it is important for a corporate communication agency to have a strong understanding of the needs and goals of clients, as well as the latest trends and best practices in the field of corporate communication.

Some actionable tips for starting a corporate communication agency in Africa include:

- Research the local market to understand the demand for corporate communication services and the competitive landscape.

- Develop a strong understanding of the needs and goals of clients, as well as the latest trends and best practices in the field of corporate communication.

- Offer a range of services to meet the needs of different clients, such as brand development and management, media relations, internal communication, and crisis communication.

- Establish clear policies and procedures for working with clients, including project scope, timelines, and pricing.

- Focus on delivering high-quality services that meet the needs and expectations of clients.

Overall, starting a corporate communication agency in Africa can be a rewarding and lucrative business opportunity for young entrepreneurs who are passionate about helping organizations communicate effectively with their stakeholders. With careful planning and a focus on delivering excellent services, you can build a successful corporate communication agency that meets the needs of clients in your community.

There are several ways that a corporate communication agency can make money in Africa:

Project-based fees: Many corporate communication agencies in Africa charge fees for their services on a project-by-project basis. This may include an upfront fee for the development of a communication strategy or campaign, as well as ongoing maintenance and support fees.

Hourly rates: Some corporate communication agencies in Africa charge clients an hourly rate for their services, which may include brand development and management, media relations, internal communication, and crisis communication.

Maintenance and support services: Corporate communication agencies in Africa may also generate revenue through maintenance and support services, such as ongoing support for clients' communication strategies and campaigns.

Reselling products or services: Corporate communication agencies in Africa may also generate revenue by reselling products or services, such as printing or design services, to clients.

Partnerships and sponsorships: Corporate communication agencies in Africa may also generate revenue through partnerships or sponsorships with other companies or organizations.

Overall, the business model for a corporate communication agency in Africa may involve a combination of these revenue streams, depending on the specific services and offerings of the agency.

Here are some services that a corporate communication agency may provide to individual and corporate clients:

- Brand development and management
- Media relations
- Public relations
- Internal communication
- Crisis communication
- Marketing and advertising
- Social media management
- Website development and design
- Event planning (Focus on pre, process and post communication)
- Advertising and marketing services
- Content creation and management
- Graphic design
- Printing services
- Video production
- Photography

- Translation services

- Digital marketing

- Search engine optimization (SEO)

- Reputation management

- Communications training and coaching

- Media training

- Market research and analysis

By Dr. Javnyuy Joybert

CHAPTER 9:

BUSINESS MODEL FOR

BRANDING AGENCY

A branding agency is a business that helps organizations develop and manage their brand identity. This may involve creating brand strategies and guidelines, designing logos and other visual assets, developing marketing and advertising campaigns, and providing other related services.

In Africa, the practical business model for a branding agency may involve working with a variety of clients, including small and medium-sized businesses, startups, and larger organizations. The agency may offer a range of services, such as brand strategy development, logo design, marketing and advertising campaigns, and website development.

To be successful in this industry, it is important for a branding agency to have a strong understanding of the needs and goals of clients, as well as the latest trends and best practices in the field of branding.

Some actionable tips for starting a branding agency in Africa include:

- Research the local market to understand the demand for branding services and the competitive landscape.

- Develop a strong understanding of the needs and goals of clients, as well as the latest trends and best practices in the field of branding.

- Offer a range of services to meet the needs of different clients, such as brand strategy development, logo design, marketing and advertising campaigns, and website development.

- Establish clear policies and procedures for working with clients, including project scope, timelines, and pricing.

- Focus on delivering high-quality services that meet the needs and expectations of clients.

Overall, starting a branding agency in Africa can be a rewarding and lucrative business opportunity for young entrepreneurs who are passionate about helping organizations develop and manage their brand identity. With careful planning and a focus on delivering excellent services, you can build a successful branding agency that meets the needs of clients in your community.

There are several ways that a branding agency can make money in Africa:

Project-based fees: Many branding agencies in Africa charge fees for their services on a project-by-project basis. This may include an upfront fee for the development of a brand strategy or campaign, as well as ongoing maintenance and support fees.

Hourly rates: Some branding agencies in Africa charge clients an hourly rate for their services, which may include brand strategy development, logo design, marketing and advertising campaigns, and website development.

Maintenance and support services: Branding agencies in Africa may also generate revenue through maintenance and support services, such as ongoing support for clients' brand strategies and campaigns.

Reselling products or services: Branding agencies in Africa may also generate revenue by reselling products or services, such as printing or design services, to clients.

Partnerships and sponsorships: Branding agencies in Africa may also generate revenue through partnerships or sponsorships with other companies or organizations.

Overall, the business model for a branding agency in Africa may involve a combination of these revenue streams, depending on the specific services and offerings of the agency.

Here are some services that a branding agency may provide to individuals and corporate institutions:

Brand strategy development: This involves creating a plan for how an organization's brand should be positioned and communicated.

Logo design: This involves creating a visual symbol or mark that represents an organization's brand.

Marketing and advertising campaigns: This involves creating and executing campaigns to promote an organization's products or services.

Website development: This involves creating and designing a website for an organization that effectively communicates its brand and showcases its products or services.

Graphic design: This involves creating visual materials, such as brochures, business cards, and other promotional materials, that support an organization's brand.

Packaging design: This involves creating packaging designs for an organization's products that align with its brand identity.

Social media management: This involves managing an organization's social media accounts and creating content that aligns with its brand identity.

Content creation and management: This involves creating written, visual, and multimedia content that supports an organization's brand and messaging.

Advertising and marketing services: This may include creating and placing ads in various media outlets, such as television, radio, print, and online.

Public relations: This involves managing an organization's relationship with the media and the public.

Market research and analysis: This involves conducting research to understand the needs and preferences of an organization's target market, and analyzing the results to inform branding and marketing strategies.

Event planning and management: This involves organizing and executing events, such as conferences, product launches, and trade shows, that support an organization's brand and messaging.

Video production: This involves creating videos that support an organization's brand and messaging, and may include promotional videos, explainer videos, and other types of content.

Photography: This involves taking photographs that support an organization's brand and messaging, and may include product photography, event photography, and other types of imagery.

Translation services: This involves translating written materials, such as marketing materials and website content, into different languages to support an organization's brand in international markets.

Digital marketing: This involves creating and executing marketing campaigns that utilize digital channels, such as social media, email, and websites, to reach and engage with customers.

Search engine optimization (SEO): This involves optimizing an organization's website and content to improve its ranking in search engine results.

Reputation management: This involves managing and protecting an organization's reputation online and in the media.

Communications training and coaching: This involves providing training and coaching to individuals or teams on how to effectively communicate an organization's brand and messaging.

<u>Media training:</u> This involves providing training to individuals or teams on how to effectively communicate with the media.

CHAPTER 10:

DIGITAL MARKETING AGENCY BUSINESS MODEL

A digital marketing agency is a business that helps organizations reach and engage with customers through digital channels, such as websites, social media, email, and mobile apps. This may involve developing and implementing marketing campaigns, creating and managing social media accounts, optimizing websites for search engines, and providing other related services.

In Africa, the practical business model for a digital marketing agency may involve working with a variety of clients, including small and medium-sized businesses, startups, and larger organizations. The agency may offer a range of services, such as website design and development, search engine optimization (SEO), social media management, email marketing, and pay-per-click (PPC) advertising.

To be successful in this industry, it is important for a digital marketing agency to have a strong understanding of the latest technologies and trends, as well as a focus on delivering measurable results for clients.

Some actionable tips for starting a digital marketing agency in Africa include:

- Research the local market to understand the demand for digital marketing services and the competitive landscape.

- Develop a strong understanding of the latest technologies and trends in the field of digital marketing.

- Offer a range of services to meet the needs of different clients, such as website design and development, SEO, social media management, email marketing, and PPC advertising.

- Establish clear policies and procedures for working with clients, including project scope, timelines, and pricing.

- Focus on delivering measurable results for clients, such as increased website traffic, higher search engine rankings, and improved social media engagement.

Overall, starting a digital marketing agency in Africa can be a rewarding and lucrative business opportunity for young entrepreneurs who are passionate about helping organizations reach and engage with customers through digital channels. With careful planning and a focus on delivering excellent services, you can build a successful digital marketing agency that meets the needs of clients in your community.

There are several ways that a digital marketing agency can make money in Africa:

Project-based fees: Many digital marketing agencies in Africa charge fees for their services on a project-by-project basis. This may include an upfront fee for the development of a marketing campaign or website, as well as ongoing maintenance and support fees.

Hourly rates: Some digital marketing agencies in Africa charge clients an hourly rate for their services, which may include website design and development, SEO, social media management, email marketing, and PPC advertising.

Maintenance and support services: Digital marketing agencies in Africa may also generate revenue through maintenance and support services, such as ongoing support for clients' marketing campaigns and websites.

<u>Reselling products or services:</u> Digital marketing agencies in Africa may also generate revenue by reselling products or services, such as hosting or cloud services, to clients.

<u>Partnerships and sponsorships:</u> Digital marketing agencies in Africa may also generate revenue through partnerships or sponsorships with other companies or organizations.

Overall, the business model for a digital marketing agency in Africa may involve a combination of these revenue streams, depending on the specific services and offerings of the agency.

Here are some services that a digital marketing agency may provide to individuals and companies:

- Website design and development
- Search engine optimization (SEO)

- Social media management

- Email marketing

- Pay-per-click (PPC) advertising

- Content marketing

- Influencer marketing

- Video marketing

- Mobile app development

- Online reputation management

- Conversion rate optimization (CRO)

- Google Ads management

- Amazon marketing

- Affiliate marketing

- E-commerce marketing

- Marketing automation

- Landing page optimization

- Local SEO

- Ad copywriting

- Remarketing

- A/B testing

- Lead generation

- Customer acquisition

- Event marketing

- Customer journey mapping

- Marketing analytics and reporting

- Marketing strategy development

- Marketing consulting

- Public relations

- Branding

- Graphic design

- Printing services

- Translation services

CHAPTER 11:

SOCIAL MEDIA MARKETING AGENCY BUSINESS MODEL

A social media marketing agency is a business that helps organizations reach and engage with customers through social media platforms, such as Facebook, Instagram, and Twitter. This may involve creating and managing social media accounts, developing and implementing marketing campaigns, creating and sharing content, and providing other related services.

In Africa, the practical business model for a social media marketing agency may involve working with a variety of clients, including small and medium-sized businesses, startups, and larger organizations. The agency may offer a range of services, such as account setup and management, content creation and curation, influencer marketing, and social media advertising.

To be successful in this industry, it is important for a social media marketing agency to have a strong understanding of the latest technologies and trends, as well as a focus on delivering measurable results for clients.

Some actionable tips for starting a social media marketing agency in Africa include:

- Research the local market to understand the demand for social media marketing services and the competitive landscape.

- Develop a strong understanding of the latest technologies and trends in the field of social media marketing.

- Offer a range of services to meet the needs of different clients, such as account setup and management, content creation and curation, influencer marketing, and social media advertising.

- Establish clear policies and procedures for working with clients, including project scope, timelines, and pricing.

- Focus on delivering measurable results for clients, such as increased website traffic, higher search engine rankings, and improved social media engagement.

Overall, starting a social media marketing agency in Africa can be a rewarding and lucrative business opportunity for young entrepreneurs who are passionate about helping organizations reach and engage with customers through social media. With careful planning and a focus on delivering excellent services, you can build a successful social media marketing agency that meets the needs of clients in your community.

There are several ways that a social media marketing agency can make money in Africa:

Project-based fees: Many social media marketing agencies in Africa charge fees for their services on a project-by-project basis. This may include an upfront fee for the development of a marketing campaign or social media account setup, as well as ongoing maintenance and support fees.

Hourly rates: Some social media marketing agencies in Africa charge clients an hourly rate for their services, which may include account setup and management, content creation and curation, influencer marketing, and social media advertising.

Maintenance and support services: Social media marketing agencies in Africa may also generate revenue through maintenance and support services, such as ongoing support for clients' social media accounts and campaigns.

Reselling products or services: Social media marketing agencies in Africa may also generate revenue by reselling products or services, such as social media tools or training, to clients.

Partnerships and sponsorships: Social media marketing agencies in Africa may also generate revenue through partnerships or sponsorships with other companies or organizations.

Overall, the business model for a social media marketing agency in Africa may involve a combination of these revenue streams, depending on the specific services and offerings of the agency.

CHAPTER 12:

CONTENT CREATION AGENCY

A content creation agency is a business that helps organizations develop and produce written, visual, and multimedia content. This may include creating articles, blog posts, social media posts, videos, graphics, and other types of content for a variety of purposes, such as marketing, branding, and communication.

In Africa, the practical business model for a content creation agency may involve working with a variety of clients, including small and medium-sized businesses, startups, and larger organizations. The agency may offer a range of services, such as content strategy development, copywriting, graphic design, video production, and social media management.

By Dr. Javnyuy Joybert

To be successful in this industry, it is important for a content creation agency to have a strong understanding of the needs and goals of clients, as well as a focus on delivering high-quality content that meets the needs of its audience.

Some actionable tips for starting a content creation agency in Africa include:

- Research the local market to understand the demand for content creation services and the competitive landscape.

- Develop a strong understanding of the needs and goals of clients, as well as the latest trends and best practices in the field of content creation.

- Offer a range of services to meet the needs of different clients, such as content strategy development, copywriting, graphic design, video production, and social media management.

- Establish clear policies and procedures for working with clients, including project scope, timelines, and pricing.

- Focus on delivering high-quality content that meets the needs and expectations of clients and their audience.

Overall, starting a content creation agency in Africa can be a rewarding and lucrative business opportunity for young entrepreneurs who are passionate about helping organizations develop and produce engaging and effective content. With careful planning and a focus on delivering excellent services, you can build a successful content creation agency that meets the needs of clients in your community.

There are several ways that a content creation agency can make money in Africa:

Project-based fees: Many content creation agencies in Africa charge fees for their services on a project-by-project basis. This may include an upfront fee for the development of a content strategy or the production of specific content, as well as ongoing maintenance and support fees.

Hourly rates: Some content creation agencies in Africa charge clients an hourly rate for their services, which may include content strategy development, copywriting, graphic design, video production, and social media management.

Maintenance and support services: Content creation agencies in Africa may also generate revenue through maintenance and support services, such as ongoing support for clients' content marketing campaigns and social media accounts.

Reselling products or services: Content creation agencies in Africa may also generate revenue by

71

reselling products or services, such as content management systems or training, to clients.

Partnerships and sponsorships: Content creation agencies in Africa may also generate revenue through partnerships or sponsorships with other companies or organizations.

Overall, the business model for a content creation agency in Africa may involve a combination of these revenue streams, depending on the specific services and offerings of the agency.

Here are some services that a content creation agency may provide to individuals and institutions:

Content strategy development: This involves creating a plan for how an organization's content will be developed, produced, and distributed.

Copywriting: This involves creating written content, such as articles, blog posts, and social media posts, for an organization.

Graphic design: This involves creating visual materials, such as infographics, logos, and other promotional materials, for an organization.

Video production: This involves creating videos for an organization, such as promotional videos, explainer videos, and other types of content.

Social media management: This involves managing an organization's social media accounts and creating content that aligns with its brand identity.

Content management: This involves organizing and managing an organization's content, including creating and updating content on websites and other platforms.

Marketing and advertising campaigns: This involves creating and executing campaigns to promote an organization's products or services.

Email marketing: This involves creating and sending email campaigns to promote an organization's products or services.

Search engine optimization (SEO): This involves optimizing an organization's content to improve its ranking in search engine results.

Public relations: This involves managing an organization's relationship with the media and the public.

Blog management: This involves creating and managing a blog for an organization, including developing and publishing blog posts, moderating comments, and promoting the blog through social media and other channels.

E-book creation: This involves creating and formatting e-books for an organization, which may be used as lead magnets, promotional materials, or other purposes.

Infographic creation: This involves creating visual representations of data or information for an organization, often in the form of an infographic.

Presentation design: This involves creating slide decks or other visual materials for presentations, such as pitch decks, company overviews, or product demonstrations.

Social media advertising: This involves creating and executing paid advertising campaigns on social media platforms to promote an organization's products or services.

Marketing automation: This involves using software and other tools to automate marketing tasks, such as email campaigns and social media posting.

Video editing: This involves editing and post-production work for videos, such as adding music, graphics, and other effects.

Translation services: This involves translating written materials, such as marketing materials and website content, into different languages to reach a wider audience.

Voiceover work: This involves creating voiceovers for videos, presentations, or other materials for an organization.

CHAPTER 13:

BOOK WRITING AND

PUBLISHING AGENCY

A book writing and publishing agency is a business that helps authors write and publish books. This may involve providing writing and editing services, as well as assisting with the publishing process, such as formatting, design, and distribution.

In Africa, the practical business model for a book writing and publishing agency may involve working with a variety of authors, including those who are self-publishing and those who are seeking traditional publishing deals. The agency may offer a range of services, such as writing coaching, editing, formatting, design, and distribution.

To be successful in this industry, it is important for a book writing and publishing agency to have a strong understanding of the publishing industry and the needs of authors, as well as a focus on delivering high-quality services.

Some actionable tips for starting a book writing and publishing agency in Africa include:

- Research the local market to understand the demand for book writing and publishing services and the competitive landscape.

- Develop a strong understanding of the publishing industry and the needs of authors, including the various options for publishing and the steps involved in the process.

- Offer a range of services to meet the needs of different authors, such as writing coaching, editing, formatting, design, and distribution.

- Establish clear policies and procedures for working with clients, including project scope, timelines, and pricing.

- Focus on delivering high-quality services that meet the needs and expectations of authors and their readers.

Overall, starting a book writing and publishing agency in Africa can be a rewarding and lucrative business opportunity for young entrepreneurs who are passionate about helping authors write and publish their books. With careful planning and a focus on delivering excellent services, you can build a successful book writing and publishing agency that meets the needs of authors in your community.

There are several ways that a book writing and publishing agency can make money in Africa:

Project-based fees: Many book writing and publishing agencies in Africa charge fees for their services on a project-by-project basis. This may include an upfront fee for writing coaching or editing services, as well as ongoing maintenance and support fees for publishing services.

Hourly rates: Some book writing and publishing agencies in Africa charge clients an hourly rate for their services, which may include writing coaching, editing, formatting, design, and distribution.

Maintenance and support services: Book writing and publishing agencies in Africa may also generate revenue through maintenance and support services, such as ongoing support for clients' publishing efforts.

Royalties: If a book writing and publishing agency in Africa helps an author secure a traditional publishing deal, the agency may receive a percentage of the royalties generated by the book sales.

Reselling products or services: Book writing and publishing agencies in Africa may also generate revenue by reselling products or services, such as writing tools or training, to clients.

Partnerships and sponsorships: Book writing and publishing agencies in Africa may also generate revenue through partnerships or sponsorships with other companies or organizations.

Overall, the business model for a book writing and publishing agency in Africa may involve a combination of these revenue streams, depending on the specific services and offerings of the agency.

Here are some services that a book writing and publishing agency may provide to individuals and institutions:

Writing coaching: This involves providing guidance and support to authors as they write their books, including helping them develop their ideas, organize their content, and improve their writing skills.

Editing: This involves reviewing and improving the content of a book, including correcting errors, improving the flow and clarity of the writing, and ensuring that the book meets industry standards.

Formatting: This involves preparing a book for publication, including designing the layout, adding graphics and other elements, and ensuring that the book is compatible with various formats and platforms.

Design: This involves creating visual elements for a book, such as the cover design, illustrations, and other graphics.

Distribution: This involves getting a book into the hands of readers, including through traditional publishing channels, self-publishing platforms, and online retailers.

Marketing and promotion: This involves helping authors promote their books and reach their target audience, including through social media, advertising, and public relations efforts.

Ghostwriting: This involves writing a book on behalf of another person, typically under their name.

Co-authoring: This involves working with another person to write a book together.

Translation services: This involves translating a book into different languages to reach a wider audience.

E-book conversion: This involves converting a physical book into an electronic format, such as a PDF or e-pub, for distribution on digital platforms.

Audiobook production: This involves creating an audiobook version of a book, which may be distributed through platforms such as Audible or ACX.

Print on demand: This involves using a service to print and fulfill orders for physical copies of a book as they are requested, rather than printing a large batch of books upfront.

Rights management: This involves managing the rights and permissions for a book, including copyright registration and licensing agreements.

Self-publishing support: This involves providing guidance and support to authors who are self-publishing their books, including assistance with formatting, design, and distribution.

<u>Traditional publishing support:</u> This involves helping authors secure traditional publishing deals and navigate the publishing process, including assistance with proposal development and agent negotiations.

<u>Manuscript evaluations:</u> This involves providing feedback and assessments of a book manuscript to help authors improve their work and increase their chances of success in the publishing industry.

Overall, a book writing and publishing agency can provide a wide range of services to help authors write, publish, and promote their books successfully.

CHAPTER 14:

ACCOUNTING AND TAX FIRM BUSINESS MODEL

An accounting and tax firm is a business that provides financial services to individuals and organizations. These services may include bookkeeping, tax preparation, financial planning, and consulting.

In Africa, there are several ways that an accounting and tax firm can make money.

Some of the most common business models for this type of firm include:

<u>Charging hourly rates for services:</u> Many accounting and tax firms charge their clients an hourly rate for the services they provide. This can

By Dr. Javnyuy Joybert

include anything from basic bookkeeping tasks to complex tax planning.

Offering fixed-price packages: Instead of charging hourly rates, some firms offer their clients fixed-price packages that include a set number of services. This can be a good option for clients who need ongoing support with their financial affairs.

Providing value-added services: In addition to traditional accounting and tax services, firms can also make money by offering value-added services such as business planning, financial modeling, and risk management.

Building relationships with referral partners: Another way that firms can make money is by building relationships with referral partners, such as attorneys, financial advisors, and other professionals who can refer clients to the firm.

Marketing to target audiences: Firms can also make money by marketing their services to specific target audiences, such as small businesses or high net worth individuals.

Some actionable tips for young entrepreneurs looking to start an accounting and tax firm in Africa include:

Build a strong team: Assemble a team of skilled professionals who can provide high-quality services to your clients.

Focus on building relationships: Building strong relationships with your clients and referral partners is key to success in this business.

Stay up to date with industry trends: Make sure to stay current with industry trends and changes in tax laws so that you can offer your clients the most relevant and valuable advice.

Invest in marketing: Investing in marketing and outreach efforts can help you attract new clients and grow your business.

In summary, an accounting and tax firm in Africa can make money by charging hourly rates or offering fixed-price packages for its services, providing value-added services, building relationships with referral partners, and marketing to target audiences. By building a strong team, focusing on relationships, staying up to date with industry trends, and investing in marketing, young entrepreneurs can successfully launch and grow their own accounting and tax firm in Africa.

Here is a list of services that an accounting and tax firm in Africa can provide to individuals and institutions:

- Bookkeeping and financial statement preparation

- Tax preparation and planning

- Payroll management

- Financial planning and budgeting

- Business consulting and advisory services

- Risk management and insurance planning

- Business valuations

- Merger and acquisition consulting

- Succession planning

- Estate planning

- Internal audit support

- Fraud examination and prevention

- Information technology consulting

- Governmental accounting and auditing

- Financial modeling and forecasting

- Business plan development

- Project management

- Performance improvement consulting

- Corporate finance services, including debt and equity financing

- International tax consulting

- Transfer pricing

- Employee benefit plan audit services

- Litigation support

- Forensic accounting

- Investment advisory services

- Retirement planning

- Asset management

- Wealth management

- Private wealth services

CHAPTER 15:

ERRAND AND DELIVERY AGENCY BUSINESS MODEL

An errand and delivery agency is a business that helps individuals and businesses by completing tasks and delivering items on their behalf. These tasks can include grocery shopping, picking up dry cleaning, or delivering documents and packages.

In Africa, an errand and delivery agency can make money in several ways:

<u>**Charging a fee for each task or delivery completed:**</u> The business can set a flat fee or hourly rate for each task or delivery they complete.

<u>**Partnering with local businesses:**</u> The business can partner with local businesses, such as

restaurants or retailers, to handle their delivery needs in exchange for a commission or fee.

Offering subscription plans: The business can offer monthly or yearly subscription plans that allow customers to request a certain number of tasks or deliveries each month at a discounted rate.

Providing additional services: The business can also offer additional services, such as packing and shipping items, or coordinating travel arrangements, for an additional fee.

To succeed in this business, it's important to offer reliable, efficient service and to build strong relationships with both customers and business partners. Marketing your services through social media, local advertising, and word-of-mouth can also help attract new clients.

Overall, an errand and delivery agency can be a lucrative business for entrepreneurs looking to provide a valuable service to busy individuals and businesses in Africa. By offering a wide range of tasks and delivery services and consistently delivering high-quality service, this business can thrive and generate significant income.

Here are some actionable tips for starting and running a successful errand and delivery agency in Africa:

Research the local market: Before starting your business, it's important to understand the needs of your target audience and identify any potential competition. This will help you tailor your services to meet the specific needs of your market and differentiate your business from others.

Choose the right business model: Decide on the best business model for your errand and delivery agency based on your target audience and the services you want to offer. This could include charging a flat fee or hourly rate, offering subscription plans, or partnering with local businesses.

Build a strong team: A reliable and efficient team is essential for running a successful errand and delivery agency. Consider hiring employees or contractors who are organized, detail-oriented, and customer-service oriented.

Invest in the right technology: Technology can help streamline your operations and improve efficiency. Consider investing in tools such as a cloud-based task management system or a delivery tracking app to help manage your business.

Market your services: It's important to get the word out about your business to attract new clients. Consider marketing your services through social media, local advertising, and word-of-mouth to reach potential customers.

With these tips in mind, you can successfully start and run a thriving errand and delivery agency in Africa, providing valuable services to individuals and businesses while generating significant income.

Here are some examples of services that an errand and delivery agency in Africa could offer to individuals and institutions:

Grocery shopping: The business can help individuals by shopping for groceries and delivering them to their home or office.

Dry cleaning and laundry: The business can pick up and deliver dry cleaning and laundry for individuals.

Personal shopping: The business can help individuals shop for clothing, gifts, or other items and deliver them to their home or office.

Document and package delivery: The business can deliver documents, packages, and other items on behalf of individuals and businesses.

Pet care: The business can offer pet-sitting and dog-walking services for individuals who are unable to care for their pets while they are away.

Event planning: The business can help individuals and businesses plan and execute events, including coordinating logistics, setting up decorations, and running errands.

Travel arrangements: The business can help individuals and businesses plan and book travel, including flights, hotels, and transportation.

Home organization: The business can help individuals declutter and organize their homes, including sorting through and disposing of items and setting up storage solutions.

Packing and shipping: The business can offer packing and shipping services for individuals and businesses, including packing items for shipping and coordinating with carriers to ensure safe and timely delivery.

Office support: The business can help businesses with tasks such as filing, data entry, and photocopying.

Professional services: The business can offer professional services, such as administrative support or virtual assistance, to individuals and businesses.

Home maintenance: The business can offer home maintenance services, such as minor repairs, cleaning, and yard work, to individuals and businesses.

Personal assistant: The business can offer personal assistant services, such as managing schedules, making appointments, and running errands, to individuals and businesses.

Home healthcare: The business can offer home healthcare services, such as medication reminders and assistance with daily activities, to individuals in need.

Party planning: The business can help individuals and businesses plan and execute parties, including coordinating logistics, setting up decorations, and running errands.

Overall, the services offered by an errand and delivery agency can vary depending on the needs of the local market and the specific capabilities and resources of the business. By offering a wide range of services and consistently delivering high-quality service, an errand and delivery agency can meet the needs of a diverse range of clients and generate significant income.

CHAPTER 16:

BUSINESS MODEL CAREER ORIENTATION AND COACHING AGENCY

A career orientation and coaching agency is a business that helps individuals explore career options and make informed decisions about their professional paths. This can include assessing strengths and weaknesses, exploring different industries and job roles, and developing job search and career advancement strategies.

In Africa, a career orientation and coaching agency can make money in several ways:

Charging a fee for individual coaching sessions: The business can charge a fee for one-on-one coaching sessions with clients to help them explore career options, develop job search strategies, and build their professional skills.

Offering group workshops and seminars: The business can offer group workshops and seminars on topics such as resume writing, interview skills, and career advancement for a fee.

Providing online courses: The business can create and sell online courses on career development topics, such as how to change careers or how to negotiate a raise.

Partnering with schools and universities: The business can partner with schools and universities to provide career coaching services to students and alumni in exchange for a fee.

Providing consulting services to businesses: The business can offer consulting services to businesses on topics such as employee development and career advancement.

To succeed in this business, it's important to have a deep understanding of the job market and the skills and experience that are in demand. It's also important to build strong relationships with clients and provide high-quality, personalized coaching and support. Marketing your services through social media, local advertising, and word-of-mouth can also help attract new clients.

Overall, a career orientation and coaching agency can be a rewarding and lucrative business for entrepreneurs looking to help individuals achieve their professional goals in Africa. By offering a range of coaching and development services and consistently delivering high-quality service, this business can thrive and generate significant income.

Here are some actionable tips for starting and running a successful career orientation and coaching agency in Africa:

Research the local job market: Before starting your business, it's important to understand the current job market in your area and identify any areas of demand or growth. This will help you tailor your services to meet the specific needs of your market and help clients make informed decisions about their careers.

Build a strong team: A knowledgeable and experienced team is essential for running a successful career orientation and coaching agency. Consider hiring or partnering with career coaches and other professionals who have a deep understanding of the job market and expertise in areas such as resume writing, interview skills, and career advancement.

Offer a range of services: To attract a diverse range of clients, it's important to offer a range of services, such as one-on-one coaching, group workshops, and online courses. This will allow you to meet the needs of a variety of clients and generate multiple streams of income.

Invest in technology: Technology can help streamline your operations and improve efficiency. Consider investing in tools such as a scheduling and payment platform to help manage your business.

Network and build partnerships: Building strong relationships with schools, universities, and businesses can be a valuable source of referrals and new clients. Consider networking and building partnerships to expand your reach and grow your business.

With these tips in mind, you can successfully start and run a thriving career orientation and coaching agency in Africa, helping individuals achieve their professional goals and generating significant income in the process.

Here are some examples of services that a career orientation and coaching agency in Africa could offer to individuals and institutions:

One-on-one career coaching: The business can offer individual coaching sessions to help clients explore career options, develop job search strategies, and build their professional skills.

Group workshops and seminars: The business can offer group workshops and seminars on topics such as resume writing, interview skills, and career advancement.

Online courses: The business can create and sell online courses on career development topics, such as how to change careers or how to negotiate a raise.

Resume and cover letter writing: The business can offer resume and cover letter writing services to help clients create professional and effective job application materials.

Interview coaching: The business can offer coaching on interview skills, including how to answer common interview questions and how to make a strong impression.

Career advancement coaching: The business can help clients develop strategies for advancing their careers, including building professional networks and negotiating promotions and salary increases.

Consulting services for businesses: The business can offer consulting services to businesses on topics such as employee development and career advancement.

Outplacement services: The business can help individuals who have been laid off or are seeking a career change by providing job search support and career coaching.

College and graduate school counseling: The business can help students explore college and graduate school options, including identifying programs that align with their career goals and helping with the application process.

Professional development workshops: The business can offer workshops and seminars on professional development topics, such as leadership skills, time management, and communication.

Executive coaching: The business can offer coaching services to executives and high-level managers to help them achieve their professional goals and advance their careers.

Career assessment and testing: The business can offer assessment tools and tests to help clients explore their strengths and interests and identify potential career paths.

Job search support: The business can help clients identify job openings, create targeted resumes and cover letters, and prepare for interviews.

CHAPTER 17:

BUSINESS TRAINING AND CONSULTING FIRM BUSINESS MODEL

A business training and consulting firm is a business that helps organizations improve their performance and achieve their goals through training and consulting services. These services can include training on management and leadership, sales and marketing, and technical skills, as well as consulting on business strategy and operations.

In Africa, a business training and consulting firm can make money in several ways:

Charging a fee for training and consulting services: The business can charge a fee for training and consulting services provided to organizations.

This can be a flat fee for a specific project or an hourly rate for ongoing support.

Selling training and consulting packages: The business can offer packages of training and consulting services at a discounted rate, allowing organizations to purchase a set of services in advance.

Offering online courses and resources: The business can create and sell online courses and resources on business-related topics, such as leadership development or marketing strategy.

Providing coaching and mentorship: The business can offer coaching and mentorship services to individuals and businesses, helping them develop their skills and achieve their goals.

Partnering with other organizations: The business can partner with other organizations, such as schools or professional associations, to provide training and consulting services in exchange for a fee.

To succeed in this business, it's important to have a deep understanding of business principles and best practices and to be able to effectively communicate and teach these concepts to others. It's also important to build strong relationships with clients and to be able to adapt to their specific needs and goals. Marketing your services through social media, local advertising, and word-of-mouth can also help attract new clients.

Overall, a business training and consulting firm can be a lucrative and rewarding business for entrepreneurs looking to help organizations improve their performance and achieve their goals in Africa. By offering a range of training and consulting services and consistently delivering high-quality service, this business can thrive and generate significant income.

Here are some actionable tips for starting and running a successful business training and consulting firm in Africa:

Identify your area of expertise: Before starting your business, it's important to identify your specific areas of expertise and the types of organizations you want to work with. This will help you tailor your services to meet the needs of your target market and differentiate your business from others.

Build a strong team: A knowledgeable and experienced team is essential for running a successful business training and consulting firm. Consider hiring or partnering with experts in various business disciplines to provide a wide range of services to your clients.

Offer a range of services: To attract a diverse range of clients, it's important to offer a range of services, such as training, consulting, coaching, and mentorship. This will allow you to meet the needs of a variety of clients and generate multiple streams of income.

Invest in technology: Technology can help streamline your operations and improve efficiency. Consider investing in tools such as a project management system or a learning management system to help manage your business.

Network and build partnerships: Building strong relationships with other organizations, such as schools, professional associations, and local businesses, can be a valuable source of referrals and new clients. Consider networking and building partnerships to expand your reach and grow your business.

With these tips in mind, you can successfully start and run a thriving business training and consulting firm in Africa, helping organizations improve their performance and achieve their goals while generating significant income in the process.

Here are a few more tips for starting and running a successful business training and consulting firm in Africa:

<u>**Stay up to date:**</u> It's important to stay current on the latest business trends and best practices in order to provide relevant and valuable services to your clients. Consider attending industry events, reading business publications, and continuously learning and developing your skills to stay ahead of the curve.

<u>**Customize your services:**</u> Each organization is unique and has specific needs and goals. It's

important to be able to customize your services to meet the needs of each client. This may involve conducting assessments to understand the organization's current challenges and opportunities and developing tailored training and consulting plans.

Foster a culture of continuous learning: Encourage a culture of continuous learning within your organization and with your clients. This may involve offering ongoing support and resources, such as follow-up coaching sessions or access to online resources, to help clients apply what they have learned and continue to grow and develop.

Measure and report on the impact of your services: Demonstrating the value and impact of your services to clients is essential for building trust and long-term relationships. Consider implementing systems to measure and report on the impact of your services, such as collecting feedback

116

from clients and tracking key performance indicators.

By offering a wide range of high-quality services and continuously learning and adapting to meet the needs of your clients, a business training and consulting firm can help organizations improve their performance and achieve their goals while generating significant income in the process.

Leadership development: The business can offer training and consulting services on leadership development, including coaching and mentorship to help individuals develop their leadership skills.

Sales and marketing training: The business can offer training and consulting services on sales and marketing strategies, including how to create and implement effective marketing plans and how to increase sales.

Technical skills training: The business can offer training on technical skills, such as computer programming or project management, to help individuals and organizations improve their performance and efficiency.

Business strategy consulting: The business can offer consulting services on business strategy, including helping organizations develop and implement plans to achieve their goals.

Operations consulting: The business can offer consulting services on business operations, including areas such as supply chain management and process improvement.

Change management: The business can offer training and consulting services on change management, including how to effectively implement and manage change within an organization.

Executive coaching: The business can offer coaching services to executives and high-level managers to help them achieve their professional goals and advance their careers.

Team building and conflict resolution: The business can offer training and consulting services on team building and conflict resolution to help organizations improve teamwork and resolve conflicts.

Employee engagement: The business can offer training and consulting services on employee engagement, including how to motivate and retain employees and how to create a positive work culture.

Time management and productivity: The business can offer training and consulting services on time management and productivity, including how to set and achieve goals, prioritize tasks, and avoid distractions.

Communication skills: The business can offer training and consulting services on communication skills, including how to effectively communicate with colleagues and clients and how to give presentations.

Financial management: The business can offer training and consulting services on financial management, including how to create and manage budgets and how to make informed financial decisions.

Business ethics: The business can offer training and consulting services on business ethics, including how to make ethical decisions and how to create a culture of integrity within an organization.

CHAPTER 18:

AUDIOVISUAL AGENCY BUSINESS MODEL

An audiovisual agency is a business that provides audiovisual services, such as video production, event planning, and audio engineering, to clients. These services can be used for a variety of purposes, including marketing, events, and entertainment.

In Africa, an audiovisual agency can make money in several ways:

Charging a fee for services: The business can charge a fee for the audiovisual services it provides to clients. This can be a flat fee for a specific project or an hourly rate for ongoing support.

Selling products: The business can sell products related to audiovisual services, such as audio equipment or video editing software.

Providing rental services: The business can offer rental services for audiovisual equipment, such as audio systems or video cameras.

Partnering with other organizations: The business can partner with other organizations, such as event planning companies or marketing agencies, to provide audiovisual services in exchange for a fee.

To succeed in this business, it's important to have a deep understanding of audiovisual technology and techniques and to be able to deliver high-quality service to clients. It's also important to build strong relationships with clients and to be able to adapt to their specific needs and goals. Marketing your

services through social media, local advertising, and word-of-mouth can also help attract new clients.

Overall, an audiovisual agency can be a lucrative and rewarding business for entrepreneurs looking to provide high-quality audiovisual services to clients in Africa. By offering a range of services and consistently delivering high-quality service, this business can thrive and generate significant income.

Here are some actionable tips for starting and running a successful audiovisual agency in Africa:

Identify your area of expertise: Before starting your business, it's important to identify your specific areas of expertise and the types of clients you want to work with. This will help you tailor your services to meet the needs of your target market and differentiate your business from others.

Build a strong team: A knowledgeable and experienced team is essential for running a successful audiovisual agency. Consider hiring or partnering with experts in various audiovisual disciplines to provide a wide range of services to your clients.

Offer a range of services: To attract a diverse range of clients, it's important to offer a range of services, such as video production, event planning, and audio engineering. This will allow you to meet the needs of a variety of clients and generate multiple streams of income.

Invest in technology: Technology is an important part of the audiovisual industry. Consider investing in the latest equipment and software to provide high-quality services to your clients.

Network and build partnerships: Building strong relationships with other organizations, such as event planning companies and marketing agencies, can be a valuable source of referrals and new clients. Consider networking and building partnerships to expand your reach and grow your business.

With these tips in mind, you can successfully start and run a thriving audiovisual agency in Africa, providing high-quality services to clients and generating significant income in the process.

<u>Stay up to date:</u> It's important to stay current on the latest audiovisual technology and techniques in order to provide relevant and valuable services to your clients. Consider attending industry events, reading industry publications, and continuously learning and developing your skills to stay ahead of the curve.

<u>Customize your services:</u> Each client is unique and has specific needs and goals. It's important to be able to customize your services to meet the needs of each client. This may involve conducting assessments to understand the client's current challenges and opportunities and developing tailored solutions.

Foster a culture of innovation: Encourage a culture of innovation within your organization and with your clients. This may involve exploring new technologies and techniques, and being open to new ideas and approaches.

Measure and report on the impact of your services: Demonstrating the value and impact of your services to clients is essential for building trust and long-term relationships. Consider implementing systems to measure and report on the impact of your services, such as collecting feedback from clients and tracking key performance indicators.

By offering a wide range of high-quality services and continuously learning and adapting to meet the needs of your clients, an audiovisual agency can help clients achieve their goals and generate significant income in the process.

Here are some examples of services that an audiovisual agency in Africa could offer to individuals and institutions:

Video production: The business can offer video production services, including filming and editing, to create promotional videos, training videos, and other types of video content for clients.

Event planning: The business can offer event planning services, including coordinating audiovisual elements for events such as conferences, concerts, and weddings.

Audio engineering: The business can offer audio engineering services, including recording, mixing, and mastering audio for music, podcasts, and other types of audio content.

Audio and visual equipment rental: The business can offer rental services for audio and visual equipment, such as microphones, speakers, and video cameras.

Video editing: The business can offer video editing services to help clients create professional and effective video content.

Animation and graphics design: The business can offer animation and graphics design services to help clients create visual content for presentations, websites, and other applications.

Audio and visual installation: The business can offer installation services for audio and visual equipment, including setting up systems for events and permanent installations in buildings.

Sound design: The business can offer sound design services, including creating and editing sound effects and music for video and audio projects.

Video game audio: The business can offer audio services for the video game industry, including creating sound effects and music for games.

Sound system design and installation: The business can offer design and installation services for sound systems, including choosing and installing appropriate audio equipment for events and permanent installations.

Audio restoration: The business can offer audio restoration services, including cleaning up and enhancing audio from old recordings or damaged media.

Voiceover recording: The business can offer voiceover recording services, including recording and editing voiceovers for videos, audio books, and other audio projects.

Audio book production: The business can offer audio book production services, including recording, editing, and mastering audio books for clients.

CHAPTER 19:

TRAVEL AND TOURISM AGENCY

A travel and tourism agency is a business that helps clients plan and book trips, including arranging flights, accommodations, and activities. This type of business can operate online or have physical locations, such as a storefront or kiosk.

In Africa, a travel and tourism agency can make money in several ways:

Charging a fee for services: The business can charge a fee for the travel planning and booking services it provides to clients. This can be a flat fee for a specific trip or a percentage of the total cost of the trip.

Selling travel insurance: The business can sell travel insurance to clients as an added service to protect against unforeseen circumstances such as trip cancellations or medical emergencies.

Earning commissions: Many travel and tourism agencies earn commissions from airlines, hotels, and other travel providers for booking trips with them. These commissions can be a significant source of income for the business.

Offering package deals: The business can create and sell package deals, which include a combination of flights, accommodations, and activities at a discounted price.

To succeed in this business, it's important to have a deep understanding of the travel industry and to be able to offer a wide range of options to clients. It's also important to build strong relationships with clients and to be able to adapt to their specific needs and preferences. Marketing your services through social media, local advertising, and word-of-mouth can also help attract new clients.

Overall, a travel and tourism agency can be a lucrative and rewarding business for entrepreneurs looking to help clients plan and book their dream vacations in Africa. By offering a range of services and consistently delivering high-quality service, this business can thrive and generate significant income.

Here are some actionable tips for starting and running a successful travel and tourism agency in Africa:

Identify your target market: Before starting your business, it's important to identify your target market and the types of trips and destinations that will appeal to them. This will help you tailor your services to meet the needs of your target market and differentiate your business from others.

Build relationships with travel providers:
Establishing strong relationships with airlines, hotels, and other travel providers is essential for running a successful travel and tourism agency. These relationships can help you negotiate discounts and secure commissions, which can be a significant source of income for your business.

Offer a range of options: To attract a diverse range of clients, it's important to offer a range of options, such as flights, accommodations, and activities, in different destinations. This will allow you to meet the needs of a variety of clients and generate multiple streams of income.

Invest in technology: Technology is an important part of the travel and tourism industry. Consider investing in a website and booking software to make it easy for clients to browse and book trips online.

<u>Network and build partnerships:</u> Building strong relationships with other organizations, such as hotels and tour operators, can be a valuable source of referrals and new clients. Consider networking and building partnerships to expand your reach and grow your business.

With these tips in mind, you can successfully start and run a thriving travel and tourism agency in Africa, helping clients plan and book their dream vacations and generating significant income in the process.

Here are some examples of services that a travel and tourism agency in Africa could offer to individuals and institutions:

<u>Flight booking:</u> The business can help clients book flights to a variety of destinations, including domestic and international flights.

Hotel booking: The business can help clients book accommodations in hotels, resorts, and other types of lodging.

Tour and activity booking: The business can help clients book tours and activities, such as sightseeing tours, adventure sports, and cultural experiences.

Package deals: The business can create and sell package deals, which include a combination of flights, accommodations, and activities at a discounted price.

Travel insurance: The business can sell travel insurance to clients to protect against unforeseen circumstances such as trip cancellations or medical emergencies.

Corporate travel planning: The business can help companies plan and book business trips for employees, including arranging flights, accommodations, and meetings.

Group travel planning: The business can help groups, such as families or organizations, plan and book group trips, including coordinating flights, accommodations, and activities for multiple people.

Overall, a travel and tourism agency can offer a wide range of services to help individuals and organizations plan and book their dream vacations. By consistently delivering high-quality service and offering a range of options, this business can generate significant income in the process.

Luxury travel planning: The business can specialize in luxury travel and offer high-end services such as private jets, luxury hotels, and exclusive experiences to affluent clients.

Adventure travel planning: The business can specialize in adventure travel and offer services such as booking safari tours, trekking expeditions, and other outdoor activities.

Cultural travel planning: The business can specialize in cultural travel and offer services such as booking tours to learn about local cultures and traditions and arranging homestays with local families.

Honeymoon planning: The business can offer specialized services for planning honeymoons, including booking romantic accommodations and activities for couples.

Cruise bookings: The business can help clients book cruises to a variety of destinations, including Caribbean, Mediterranean, and other popular cruise destinations.

CHAPTER 20:

AFTERSCHOOL TEACHING AGENCY

An afterschool teaching agency is a business that provides afterschool education and enrichment programs to students. These programs can include tutoring, homework help, and extracurricular activities, such as art, music, or sports.

In Africa, an afterschool teaching agency can make money in several ways:

Charging tuition fees: The business can charge tuition fees for students to participate in afterschool programs. This can be a flat fee for a specific program or a monthly fee for ongoing support.

Selling educational materials: The business can sell educational materials, such as textbooks, workbooks, and other resources, to students and parents.

Offering specialized services: The business can offer specialized services, such as test preparation or language instruction, for an additional fee.

Partnering with schools: The business can partner with schools to provide afterschool programs, in exchange for a fee or commission.

To succeed in this business, it's important to have a deep understanding of educational pedagogy and to be able to deliver high-quality instruction to students. It's also important to build strong relationships with students and parents and to be able to adapt to their specific needs and goals. Marketing your services through social media, local advertising, and word-of-mouth can also help attract new clients.

Overall, an afterschool teaching agency can be a lucrative and rewarding business for entrepreneurs looking to provide high-quality education and enrichment programs to students in Africa. By offering a range of services and consistently delivering high-quality instruction, this business can thrive and generate significant income.

Here are some actionable tips for starting and running a successful afterschool teaching agency in Africa:

Identify your area of expertise: Before starting your business, it's important to identify your specific areas of expertise and the types of students you want to work with. This will help you tailor your services to meet the needs of your target market and differentiate your business from others.

Build a strong team: A knowledgeable and experienced team is essential for running a successful afterschool teaching agency. Consider hiring or partnering with experts in various educational disciplines to provide a wide range of services to your students.

Offer a range of services: To attract a diverse range of students, it's important to offer a range of services, such as tutoring, homework help, and extracurricular activities. This will allow you to meet the needs of a variety of students and generate multiple streams of income.

Invest in technology: Technology can be an important part of the afterschool teaching industry. Consider investing in the latest educational software and tools to enhance your services and make it easier for students to learn.

Network and build partnerships: Building strong relationships with other organizations, such as schools and community centers, can be a valuable source of referrals and new clients. Consider networking and building partnerships to expand your reach and grow your business.

With these tips in mind, you can successfully start and run a thriving afterschool teaching agency in Africa, providing high-quality education and enrichment programs to students and generating significant income in the process.

Here are some examples of services that an afterschool teaching agency in Africa could offer to students and parents:

Tutoring: The business can offer one-on-one or group tutoring services to help students improve their academic skills and knowledge in a particular subject.

Homework help: The business can offer homework help services to assist students with their assignments and improve their understanding of course material.

Extracurricular activities: The business can offer extracurricular activities, such as art, music, or sports, to provide students with additional educational and enrichment opportunities.

Test preparation: The business can offer test preparation services, including test-taking strategies and practice exams, to help students perform their best on exams.

Language instruction: The business can offer language instruction, including courses in languages such as French, Spanish, or Chinese, to help students learn a new language.

Summer programs: The business can offer summer programs, such as academic camps or enrichment activities, to provide students with educational opportunities during the summer break.

Online tutoring: The business can offer online tutoring services, using video conferencing and other technology, to provide students with the convenience of receiving tutoring from anywhere.

Study skills workshops: The business can offer study skills workshops, including time management and organization strategies, to help students improve their academic performance.

College admissions assistance: The business can offer college admissions assistance, including help with the application process, essay writing, and test preparation, to help students get into their dream colleges.

Private music lessons: The business can offer private music lessons, including instruction in instruments such as guitar, piano, or voice, to help students develop their musical skills.

Sports training: The business can offer sports training, including individual or group coaching sessions, to help students improve their athletic skills.

By offering a wide range of high-quality afterschool education and enrichment services and continuously learning and adapting to meet the needs of your clients, an afterschool teaching agency can help students and parents enhance their education and enrichment opportunities, generating significant income in the process.

CHAPTER 21:

DIGITAL SKILLS TRAINING ACADEMY BUSINESS

A digital skills training academy is a business that provides training and education in various digital skills, such as computer programming, web development, and graphic design. This type of business can operate online or have physical locations, such as a classroom or training center.

In Africa, a digital skills training academy can make money in several ways:

Charging tuition fees: The business can charge tuition fees for students to participate in digital skills training programs. This can be a flat fee for a specific course or a monthly fee for ongoing training.

Selling educational materials: The business can sell educational materials, such as textbooks, workbooks, and other resources, to students and businesses.

Offering specialized training: The business can offer specialized training, such as certification programs or in-depth workshops, for an additional fee.

Providing corporate training: The business can offer digital skills training to companies and organizations, in exchange for a fee or commission.

To succeed in this business, it's important to have a deep understanding of digital skills and to be able to deliver high-quality instruction to students. It's also important to build strong relationships with students and businesses and to be able to adapt to their specific needs and goals. Marketing your

services through social media, local advertising, and word-of-mouth can also help attract new clients.

Overall, a digital skills training academy can be a lucrative and rewarding business for entrepreneurs looking to provide high-quality education and training in digital skills to individuals and organizations in Africa. By offering a range of services and consistently delivering high-quality instruction, this business can thrive and generate significant income.

Here are some actionable tips for starting and running a successful digital skills training academy in Africa:

Identify your areas of expertise: Before starting your business, it's important to identify your specific areas of expertise and the types of students or businesses you want to work with. This will help you tailor your services to meet the needs of your target market and differentiate your business from others.

Build a strong team: A knowledgeable and experienced team is essential for running a successful digital skills training academy. Consider hiring or partnering with experts in various digital disciplines to provide a wide range of services to your clients.

Offer a range of services: To attract a diverse range of clients, it's important to offer a range of services, such as computer programming, web development, and graphic design. This will allow you to meet the needs of a variety of clients and generate multiple streams of income.

Invest in technology: Technology is an important part of the digital skills training industry. Consider investing in the latest educational software and tools to enhance your services and make it easier for students to learn.

Network and build partnerships: Building strong relationships with other organizations, such as schools and tech companies, can be a valuable source of referrals and new clients. Consider networking and building partnerships to expand your reach and grow your business.

With these tips in mind, you can successfully start and run a thriving digital skills training academy in Africa, providing high-quality education and training in digital skills to individuals and organizations and generating significant income in the process.

Here are some examples of services and skills that a digital skills training academy in Africa could offer to individuals and institutions:

Computer programming: The business can offer courses and training in computer programming languages, such as Python, Java, and C++, to help students develop their programming skills.

Web development: The business can offer courses and training in web development technologies, such as HTML, CSS, and JavaScript, to help students develop their web development skills.

Graphic design: The business can offer courses and training in graphic design software, such as Adobe Photoshop, Illustrator, and InDesign, to help students develop their graphic design skills.

Data analysis: The business can offer courses and training in data analysis tools, such as Excel and SQL, to help students develop their data analysis skills.

Digital marketing: The business can offer courses and training in digital marketing, including search engine optimization (SEO), social media marketing, and email marketing, to help students develop their digital marketing skills.

Cybersecurity: The business can offer courses and training in cybersecurity, including network security and data protection, to help students develop their cybersecurity skills.

Mobile app development: The business can offer courses and training in mobile app development, including programming languages such as Swift and Kotlin, to help students develop their mobile app development skills.

Game development: The business can offer courses and training in game development, including programming languages such as C# and

Unity, to help students develop their game development skills.

CHAPTER 22:

SOFT SKILLS TRAINING ACADEMY BUSINESS MODEL

A soft skills training academy is a business that provides training and education in various soft skills, such as communication, teamwork, and leadership. This type of business can operate online or have physical locations, such as a classroom or training center.

In Africa, a soft skills training academy can make money in several ways:

Charging tuition fees: The business can charge tuition fees for students or professionals to participate in soft skills training programs. This can be a flat fee for a specific course or a monthly fee for ongoing training.

Selling educational materials: The business can sell educational materials, such as textbooks, workbooks, and other resources, to students and businesses.

Offering specialized training: The business can offer specialized training, such as certification programs or in-depth workshops, for an additional fee.

Providing corporate training: The business can offer soft skills training to companies and organizations, in exchange for a fee or commission.

To succeed in this business, it's important to have a deep understanding of soft skills and to be able to deliver high-quality instruction to students or professionals. It's also important to build strong relationships with clients and to be able to adapt to their specific needs and goals. Marketing your

services through social media, local advertising, and word-of-mouth can also help attract new clients.

Overall, a soft skills training academy can be a lucrative and rewarding business for entrepreneurs looking to provide high-quality education and training in soft skills to individuals and organizations in Africa. By offering a range of services and consistently delivering high-quality instruction, this business can thrive and generate significant income.

Here are some actionable tips for starting and running a successful soft skills training academy in Africa:

<u>Identify your areas of expertise:</u> Before starting your business, it's important to identify your specific areas of expertise and the types of students or businesses you want to work with. This will help you tailor your services to meet the needs of your target market and differentiate your business from others.

Build a strong team: A knowledgeable and experienced team is essential for running a successful soft skills training academy. Consider hiring or partnering with experts in various soft skills disciplines to provide a wide range of services to your clients.

Offer a range of services: To attract a diverse range of clients, it's important to offer a range of services, such as communication, teamwork, and leadership. This will allow you to meet the needs of a variety of clients and generate multiple streams of income.

Invest in technology: Technology can be an important part of the soft skills training industry. Consider investing in the latest educational software and tools to enhance your services and make it easier for students or professionals to learn.

<u>Network and build partnerships:</u> Building strong relationships with other organizations, such as schools and businesses, can be a valuable source of referrals and new clients. Consider networking and building partnerships to expand your reach and grow your business.

With these tips in mind, you can successfully start and run a thriving soft skills training academy in Africa, providing high-quality education and training in soft skills to individuals and organizations and generating significant income in the process.

Here are some examples of services and skills that a soft skills training academy in Africa could offer to individuals and institutions:

Communication: The business can offer courses and training in communication, including verbal, nonverbal, and written communication, to help students or professionals improve their communication skills.

Teamwork: The business can offer courses and training in teamwork, including conflict resolution, collaboration, and problem-solving, to help students or professionals improve their teamwork skills.

Leadership: The business can offer courses and training in leadership, including decision-making, delegation, and motivation, to help students or professionals develop their leadership skills.

Time management: The business can offer courses and training in time management, including setting goals, prioritizing tasks, and avoiding distractions, to help students or professionals improve their time management skills.

Stress management: The business can offer courses and training in stress management, including techniques for reducing stress, such as relaxation and mindfulness, to help students or professionals manage stress more effectively.

Interpersonal skills: The business can offer courses and training in interpersonal skills, including conflict resolution, empathy, and active listening, to help students or professionals improve their interpersonal skills.

Negotiation: The business can offer courses and training in negotiation, including strategies for negotiating salaries, contracts, and other agreements, to help students or professionals improve their negotiation skills.

Public speaking: The business can offer courses and training in public speaking, including techniques for effective presentation, to help students or professionals improve their public speaking skills.

Customer service: The business can offer courses and training in customer service, including techniques for handling customer complaints, to help students or professionals improve their customer service skills.

Networking: The business can offer courses and training in networking, including strategies for building relationships and making connections, to help students or professionals improve their networking skills:

- Emotional intelligence

- Resilience

- Empathy

- Active listening

- Assertiveness

- Emotional control

- Persuasion

- Social skills

- Motivation

- Professionalism

- Creativity

- Adaptability

- Problem-solving

- Critical thinking

- Conflict resolution

CHAPTER 23:

RESEARCH, DATA COLLECTION & ANALYSIS AGENCY

A research, data collection, and analysis agency is a business that provides research and data services to clients, including collecting and analyzing data, conducting surveys, and providing insights and recommendations based on the data. This type of business can operate online or have physical locations, such as an office or research facility.

In Africa, a research, data collection, and analysis agency can make money in several ways:

Charging fees for research and data services:

The business can charge fees for its research and data services, such as data collection, analysis, and reporting. These fees can be based on a flat rate or an hourly rate, depending on the complexity of the project.

Selling data and insights: The business can sell data and insights to clients, such as businesses or government agencies, who are interested in using the data for their own purposes.

Providing consulting services: The business can offer consulting services, such as providing recommendations or strategic planning based on the data collected and analyzed, for an additional fee.

To succeed in this business, it's important to have strong research and data analysis skills and to be able to deliver high-quality, accurate, and reliable research and data services to clients. It's also important to build strong relationships with clients and to be able to adapt to their specific needs and goals. Marketing your services through social media, local advertising, and word-of-mouth can also help attract new clients.

Overall, a research, data collection, and analysis agency can be a lucrative and rewarding business for entrepreneurs looking to provide high-quality research and data services to clients in Africa. By offering a range of services and consistently delivering high-quality research and data analysis, this business can thrive and generate significant income.

Actionable tips for starting and running a successful research, data collection, and analysis agency in Africa:

<u>**Identify your areas of expertise:**</u> Before starting your business, it's important to identify your specific areas of expertise and the types of clients you want to work with. This will help you tailor

your services to meet the needs of your target market and differentiate your business from others.

Build a strong team: A knowledgeable and experienced team is essential for running a successful research, data collection, and analysis agency. Consider hiring or partnering with experts in various research and data analysis disciplines to provide a wide range of services to your clients.

Offer a range of services: To attract a diverse range of clients, it's important to offer a range of services, such as data collection, analysis, and reporting. This will allow you to meet the needs of a variety of clients and generate multiple streams of income.

Invest in technology: Technology can be an important part of the research, data collection, and analysis industry. Consider investing in the latest research and data analysis software and tools to enhance your services and make it easier for clients to access and analyze the data.

Network and build partnerships: Building strong relationships with other organizations, such as research firms and businesses, can be a valuable source of referrals and new clients. Consider networking and building partnerships to expand your reach and grow your business.

With these tips in mind, you can successfully start and run a thriving research, data collection, and analysis agency in Africa, providing high-quality research and data services to clients and generating significant income in the process.

Here are some examples of services that a research, data collection, and analysis agency in Africa could provide to individuals and institutions:

Data collection: The business can collect data from various sources, such as online surveys, focus groups, and interviews, and use this data to generate insights and recommendations for clients.

Data analysis: The business can analyze data using statistical software and other tools to identify patterns, trends, and relationships in the data.

Reporting: The business can provide clients with reports based on the data collected and analyzed, including insights, recommendations, and visualizations of the data.

Consulting: The business can offer consulting services, such as providing recommendations or strategic planning based on the data collected and analyzed.

Survey design: The business can design surveys and other research instruments to collect data from specific populations or groups.

By offering a wide range of high-quality research and data services and continuously learning and adapting to meet the needs of your clients, a research, data collection, and analysis agency can help individuals and organizations better understand their markets and make informed decisions, generating significant income in the process.

Data visualization: The business can create visualizations of data, such as charts, graphs, and maps, to help clients understand and analyze the data more effectively.

Data management: The business can help clients manage their data, including organizing, storing, and backing up data to ensure it is secure and accessible.

Market research: The business can conduct market research to help clients understand their target markets and make informed decisions about their products or services.

Customer research: The business can conduct research to understand customer needs, preferences, and behaviors, and provide insights and recommendations to clients.

Social media analysis: The business can analyze social media data to understand trends, sentiments, and behaviors, and provide insights and recommendations to clients.

CHAPTER 24:

SOFTWARE AS A SERVICE SALES AGENCY BUSINESS MODEL

A Software as a Service (SaaS) Sales Agency Business is a company that sells software that is delivered over the internet, rather than being installed on a local computer or server. The business model for a SaaS Sales Agency in Africa is fairly straightforward: the company sells subscriptions to its software to customers in exchange for a monthly or annual fee.

There are several ways that a SaaS Sales Agency Business can make money in Africa:

<u>Sell subscriptions to individual customers:</u> This is the most common way that SaaS companies make money. Customers pay a monthly or annual

fee to use the software, and the company generates revenue based on the number of subscribers it has.

Sell subscriptions to businesses: Many businesses use SaaS software to manage their operations, and a SaaS Sales Agency can sell subscriptions to these businesses. This can be a lucrative market, as businesses are often willing to pay more for software that can help them streamline their operations and increase efficiency.

Sell additional services or products: Some SaaS companies also make money by selling additional services or products to their customers. For example, a company might offer training or consulting services to help customers get the most out of their software.

Offer a freemium model: Some SaaS companies offer a basic version of their software for free, with the option for users to upgrade to a paid version with additional features. This can be a good way to attract a large user base, as people are often willing to try out free software before committing to a paid subscription.

Here are a few actionable tips for starting a SaaS Sales Agency Business in Africa:

Find a niche market: There are many different types of software that companies and individuals might need, so it's important to find a specific niche market that you can focus on. This will help you stand out from the competition and make it easier to target your marketing efforts.

Build a strong marketing strategy: In order to attract customers, you'll need to have a strong marketing strategy in place. This might involve building a website, creating social media accounts, and running online advertising campaigns.

<u>Offer excellent customer support:</u> SaaS customers will often have questions or need help using the software, so it's important to offer excellent customer support. This might involve providing online documentation, offering training sessions, or having a dedicated customer support team available to answer questions.

<u>Continuously improve your product:</u> In order to keep your customers happy and retain their business, it's important to continuously improve your software. This might involve adding new features, fixing bugs, or making the software easier to use.

Overall, a SaaS Sales Agency Business can be a lucrative and rewarding venture in Africa, provided that you are able to identify a target market, build a strong marketing strategy, offer excellent customer support, and continuously improve your product. With the right approach, you can build a successful and sustainable business in this exciting and rapidly-growing industry.

To continue, it's also important to have a solid business plan in place. This should include a detailed financial plan, as well as a marketing and sales strategy. You'll also need to consider the logistics of delivering your software to customers, including any technical infrastructure you'll need to set up.

Another key factor in the success of a SaaS Sales Agency Business is the pricing of your software. It's important to find the right balance between making your software affordable for customers, while still generating enough revenue to sustain and grow your business. You might consider offering different pricing tiers or packages to appeal to different types of customers.

Finally, it's important to continually evaluate and assess your business model to make sure it is working effectively. This might involve analyzing customer data, tracking your sales and revenue, and making adjustments to your marketing and sales strategies as needed.

In summary, starting a SaaS Sales Agency Business in Africa can be a rewarding and lucrative venture, provided that you are able to identify a target market, build a strong marketing and sales strategy, offer excellent customer support, continuously improve your product, and have a solid business plan in place. With the right approach and hard work, you can build a successful and sustainable business in this exciting and rapidly-growing industry.

CHAPTER 25:

AFFILIATE MARKETING AGENCY BUSINESS MODEL

An Affiliate Marketing Agency Business is a company that helps businesses promote their products or services through affiliates, who are paid a commission for each sale they generate. The business model for an Affiliate Marketing Agency in Africa is fairly straightforward: the agency helps businesses find affiliates and manage their affiliate marketing programs, and in return, the agency is paid a fee or commission for its services.

There are several ways that an Affiliate Marketing Agency Business can make money in Africa:

Commission-based fee structure: Many affiliate marketing agencies charge a commission on the sales that affiliates generate. This can be a percentage of the sale price, or a fixed fee per sale.

Management fees: Some affiliate marketing agencies charge a management fee to oversee an affiliate marketing program. This might include tasks such as recruiting affiliates, managing the affiliate program, and tracking sales and commissions.

Advertising and marketing services: Some affiliate marketing agencies also offer additional services such as advertising and marketing, which can generate additional revenue.

Consulting and training: Some agencies offer consulting or training services to help businesses improve their affiliate marketing programs.

Here are a few actionable tips for starting an Affiliate Marketing Agency Business in Africa:

Build a network of affiliates: In order to be successful as an affiliate marketing agency, you'll need to build a network of affiliates who are willing to promote your clients' products or services. This might involve recruiting affiliates through various channels, such as social media, online forums, or affiliate networks.

Offer a range of services: To differentiate your business from the competition, it can be helpful to offer a range of services beyond just managing affiliate programs. This might include advertising, marketing, consulting, or training services.

Be responsive to customer needs: As an affiliate marketing agency, your success will depend on the success of your clients' affiliate programs. It's important to be responsive to their needs and help them achieve their goals, whether that means recruiting new affiliates, improving their marketing efforts, or troubleshooting any issues that arise.

Stay up-to-date on industry trends: The affiliate marketing industry is constantly evolving, so it's important to stay up-to-date on the latest trends and best practices. This might involve attending industry conferences, reading industry publications, or networking with other professionals.

Overall, an Affiliate Marketing Agency Business can be a lucrative and rewarding venture in Africa, provided that you are able to build a strong network of affiliates, offer a range of services, be responsive to customer needs, and stay up-to-date on industry trends. With the right approach and hard work, you can build a successful and sustainable business in this exciting and rapidly-growing industry.

CHAPTER 26:

DIRECT MARKETING AND SALES AGENCY BUSINESS MODEL

A Direct Marketing and Sales Agency Business is a company that helps businesses promote and sell their products or services directly to consumers. The business model for a Direct Marketing and Sales Agency in Africa is fairly straightforward: the agency helps businesses reach potential customers and generate sales, and in return, the agency is paid a fee or commission for its services.

There are several ways that a Direct Marketing and Sales Agency Business can make money in Africa:

<u>Commission-based fee structure:</u> Many direct marketing and sales agencies charge a commission on the sales that they generate for their clients. This

can be a percentage of the sale price, or a fixed fee per sale.

Management fees: Some agencies charge a management fee to oversee a direct marketing or sales campaign. This might include tasks such as developing marketing materials, managing sales efforts, and tracking results.

Advertising and marketing services: Some direct marketing and sales agencies also offer additional services such as advertising and marketing, which can generate additional revenue.

Consulting and training: Some agencies offer consulting or training services to help businesses improve their direct marketing and sales efforts.

Actionable tips for starting a Direct Marketing and Sales Agency Business in Africa:

Develop a strong marketing strategy: In order to generate sales for your clients, you'll need to have a strong marketing strategy in place. This might involve developing marketing materials, running advertising campaigns, or using social media to reach potential customers.

Recruit and Train your sales team: To be successful in direct marketing and sales, you'll need to have a skilled and knowledgeable sales team. Consider offering training and development opportunities to help your team improve their sales skills and knowledge.

Be responsive to customer needs: As a direct marketing and sales agency, your success will depend on your ability to meet the needs of your clients and their customers. It's important to be responsive to customer inquiries and concerns, and to work with your clients to develop customized solutions to meet their specific needs.

<u>Stay up-to-date on industry trends:</u> The direct marketing and sales industry is constantly evolving, so it's important to stay up-to-date on the latest trends and best practices. This might involve attending industry conferences, reading industry publications, or networking with other professionals.

Overall, a Direct Marketing and Sales Agency Business can be a lucrative and rewarding venture in Africa, provided that you are able to develop a strong marketing strategy, train your sales team, be responsive to customer needs, and stay up-to-date on industry trends. With the right approach and hard work, you can build a successful and sustainable business in this exciting and rapidly-growing industry.

CHAPTER 27:

HOUSE & OFFICE DECORATION AGENCY BUSINESS MODEL

A House & Office Decoration Agency Business is a company that helps clients decorate and furnish their homes and offices. The business model for a House & Office Decoration Agency in Africa is fairly straightforward: the agency provides decorating and furnishing services to clients in exchange for a fee.

There are several ways that a House & Office Decoration Agency Business can make money in Africa:

<u>Hourly or per project fees:</u> Many decoration agencies charge an hourly rate or a flat fee for their services. This might include tasks such as designing and planning the decoration, sourcing and

186

purchasing furnishings and materials, and implementing the decorating plan.

Retail sales: Some decoration agencies also generate revenue by selling furnishings and decor items to their clients. This might include items such as furniture, artwork, and home decor accessories.

Consulting and design services: Some agencies offer consulting and design services to help clients develop a decorating plan and style. This might involve creating mood boards, sketching out design concepts, or providing color consultations.

Home staging: Some agencies also offer home staging services to help clients prepare their homes for sale. This might involve rearranging and styling existing furnishings, or bringing in additional items to make the home more appealing to potential buyers.

Here are a few actionable tips for starting a House & Office Decoration Agency Business in Africa:

Develop a unique style and aesthetic: To stand out from the competition, it's important to have a unique style and aesthetic that sets you apart. This might involve specializing in a particular decorating style, such as modern, minimalist, or bohemian.

Build a strong portfolio: To attract clients, you'll need to have a strong portfolio of past projects to showcase your skills and style. Consider taking photos of your completed projects and creating a website or social media account to share your work.

Offer a range of services: To appeal to a wide range of clients, it can be helpful to offer a range of services beyond just decorating and furnishing. This might include consulting and design services, home staging, or retail sales.

<u>Be responsive to customer needs:</u> As a decoration agency, your success will depend on your ability to meet the needs and preferences of your clients. It's important to be responsive to their requests and to work with them to create a space that they will love.

Overall, a House & Office Decoration Agency Business can be a lucrative and rewarding venture in Africa, provided that you are able to develop a unique style and aesthetic, build a strong portfolio, offer a range of services, and be responsive to customer needs. With the right approach and hard work, you can build a successful and sustainable business in this exciting and creative industry.

CHAPTER 28:

PERSONAL FINANCE TRAINING & COACHING FIRM BUSINESS MODEL

A Personal Finance Training & Coaching Firm Business is a company that provides training and coaching services to help individuals improve their financial literacy and money management skills. The business model for a Personal Finance Training & Coaching Firm in Africa is fairly straightforward: the firm provides training and coaching services to clients in exchange for a fee.

There are several ways that a Personal Finance Training & Coaching Firm Business can make money in Africa:

Training and coaching fees: The primary way that a Personal Finance Training & Coaching Firm makes money is by charging fees for its training and coaching services. These fees might be charged on a per-hour or per-session basis, or as part of a package of services.

Course and workshop fees: Some firms also offer courses or workshops on personal finance topics, which can be a good way to reach a larger audience and generate additional revenue.

Consulting and advisory services: Some firms offer consulting or advisory services to help individuals or families with specific financial challenges or goals. This might involve creating financial plans, analyzing investment portfolios, or providing guidance on budgeting and debt management.

Product sales: Some firms also generate revenue by selling financial products, such as books, courses, or software.

Here are a few actionable tips for starting a Personal Finance Training & Coaching Firm Business in Africa:

Build your expertise: To be successful in this field, it's important to have a deep understanding of personal finance topics and to be able to effectively communicate this knowledge to others. Consider obtaining relevant certifications, such as a Certified Financial Planner (CFP) designation, or pursuing additional education and training in personal finance.

Develop a unique approach: To stand out from the competition, it's helpful to have a unique approach or niche within the personal finance industry. This might involve specializing in a

192

particular topic, such as budgeting for millennials, or focusing on a specific demographic, such as small business owners.

Market your services: To attract clients, you'll need to have a strong marketing plan in place. This might involve building a website, creating social media accounts, running online advertising campaigns, or networking with potential clients.

Offer a range of services: To appeal to a wide range of clients, it can be helpful to offer a range of services beyond just training and coaching. This might include consulting and advisory services, courses and workshops, or product sales.

Overall, a Personal Finance Training & Coaching Firm Business can be a lucrative and rewarding venture in Africa, provided that you are able to build your expertise, develop a unique approach, market your services, and offer a range of services.

With the right approach and hard work, you can build a successful and sustainable business in this growing and important industry.

Personal Finance Training & Coaching Firms typically provide a range of services to help individuals improve their financial literacy and money management skills. These services might include:

Financial planning: This might involve creating a financial plan to help individuals achieve their financial goals, such as saving for retirement or paying off debt.

Budgeting and debt management: Personal finance trainers and coaches can help individuals create a budget and develop strategies for managing and paying off debt.

Investment guidance: Some firms offer guidance on investing, including helping individuals choose the right investment products and strategies for their goals and risk tolerance.

Education and training: Many personal finance firms offer courses, workshops, or individual training sessions on topics such as budgeting, saving, investing, and debt management.

Consulting and advisory services: Some firms offer consulting or advisory services to help individuals or families with specific financial challenges or goals. This might involve analyzing investment portfolios, providing guidance on retirement planning, or helping to create a financial plan.

Product sales: Some firms also generate revenue by selling financial products, such as books, courses, or software.

Tax planning: Some firms offer guidance on tax planning, including helping individuals minimize their tax liability and maximize their tax deductions and credits.

Estate planning: Some firms offer assistance with estate planning, including creating wills, trusts, and other legal documents to ensure that individuals' assets are distributed according to their wishes after they pass away.

Insurance planning: Personal finance trainers and coaches can help individuals understand the different types of insurance they need, such as health insurance, life insurance, and disability insurance, and assist them in choosing appropriate coverage.

Credit counseling: Some firms offer credit counseling services to help individuals improve their credit scores and manage their credit accounts effectively.

Retirement planning: Personal finance trainers and coaches can help individuals plan for retirement, including developing a savings plan, choosing the right investment products, and creating a retirement budget.

Business finance: Some firms also offer training and coaching for small business owners, helping them to understand financial concepts such as cash flow management, financial planning, and tax planning.

By Dr. Javnyuy Joybert

CHAPTER 29:

VOCATIONAL TRAINING

INSTITUTE BUSINESS MODEL

A Vocational Training Institute Business is a company that provides training in specific trade or technical skills. The business model for a Vocational Training Institute in Africa is fairly straightforward: the institute provides training programs to students in exchange for tuition fees.

There are several ways that a Vocational Training Institute Business can make money in Africa:

Tuition fees: The primary source of revenue for a Vocational Training Institute is tuition fees charged to students for their training programs. These fees might be charged on a per-course or per-program basis.

Government funding (subventions): Some vocational training institutes also receive funding from government agencies or vocational training programs, which can help to support their operations.

Corporate training: Some institutes offer customized training programs to businesses or organizations, which can generate additional revenue.

Sales of training materials: Some institutes generate revenue by selling training materials, such as textbooks, manuals, or software, to students.

Here are a few actionable tips for starting a Vocational Training Institute Business in Africa:

Identify a market need: To be successful as a vocational training institute, it's important to identify a market need and offer training programs that meet that need. This might involve researching industry trends and workforce demand, and designing programs that address specific skills shortages or job market needs.

Develop high-quality curricula: To attract and retain students, it's important to offer high-quality training programs that are relevant and effective. Consider working with industry experts to develop your curricula and ensure that your programs are up-to-date and meet industry standards.

Market your programs: To attract students, you'll need to have a strong marketing plan in place. This might involve building a website, creating social media accounts, running online advertising campaigns, or networking with potential students and employers.

Offer a range of services: To appeal to a wide range of students, it can be helpful to offer a range of training programs and services. This might include short-term courses, long-term programs online courses, corporate training, or sales of training materials.

Foster partnerships: To strengthen your institute and provide additional opportunities for your students, it can be helpful to forge partnerships with local businesses, organizations, and other vocational training institutes. These partnerships might involve internships, job placements, or collaborative projects.

Overall, a Vocational Training Institute Business can be a lucrative and rewarding venture in Africa, provided that you are able to identify a market need, develop high-quality curricula, market your programs, offer a range of services, and foster partnerships. With the right approach and hard work, you can build a successful and sustainable business in this important and growing industry.

Vocational Training Institutes in Africa can offer a wide range of training programs in various trade and technical skills.

Here are a few examples:

Construction and carpentry: Training in construction and carpentry skills can include programs in building design, construction technology, and carpentry techniques.

Automotive repair: Vocational training institutes can offer programs in automotive repair and maintenance, including training in engine repair, transmission repair, and brake and suspension work.

Culinary arts: Institutes can offer training in culinary arts, including cooking techniques, food safety, and restaurant management.

Computer and IT: Institutes can offer training programs in computer and information technology fields such as programming, network administration, and database management.

Cosmetology: Institutes can offer training programs in cosmetology and beauty services, including hair styling, makeup artistry, and nail technology.

Electrician: Institutes can offer training programs in electrical work, including electrical installation and repair.

Plumbing: Institutes can offer training programs in plumbing, including installation and repair of plumbing systems.

HVAC: Institutes can offer training programs in heating, ventilation, and air conditioning (HVAC) systems, including installation and repair.

Welding: Institutes can offer training programs in welding and metal fabrication, including training in different welding techniques and safety practices.

Agriculture and forestry: Institutes can offer training programs in agriculture and forestry, including training in animal care, crop production, and forestry management.

Graphic design: Institutes can offer training programs in graphic design, including training in design software and techniques such as Photoshop and Illustrator.

Industrial machinery: Institutes can offer training programs in the operation and maintenance of industrial machinery, such as CNC machines and lathes.

Landscaping and horticulture: Institutes can offer training programs in landscaping and horticulture, including training in plant care, garden design, and irrigation systems.

Manufacturing: Institutes can offer training programs in manufacturing, including training in assembly line work, quality control, and machine operation.

Photography: Institutes can offer training programs in photography, including training in camera operation, lighting techniques, and photo editing software.

Retail and customer service: Institutes can offer training programs in retail and customer service, including training in sales techniques, customer service skills, and inventory management.

Textile and fashion: Institutes can offer training programs in textile and fashion, including training in sewing, design, and fashion marketing.

Transportation: Institutes can offer training programs in transportation, including training in truck driving, logistics, and transportation safety.

Veterinary technician: Institutes can offer training programs in veterinary technician skills, including training in animal care and handling

CHAPTER 30:

PRIVATE AMBULANCE SERVICES BUSINESS MODEL

A Private Ambulance Services Business is a company that provides medical transportation services to individuals in need of medical care. The business model for a Private Ambulance Services Business in Africa is fairly straightforward: the business provides ambulance services to clients in exchange for a fee.

There are several ways that a Private Ambulance Services Business can make money in Africa:

Transport fees: The primary way that a Private Ambulance Services Business makes money is by charging fees for its transportation services. These fees might be based on the distance traveled, the type of vehicle used, or the level of medical care required.

Insurance billing: Some Private Ambulance Services Businesses also bill insurance companies for their services, provided that the patient has coverage.

Contract work: Some businesses enter into contracts with hospitals, nursing homes, or other healthcare providers to provide transportation services on a regular basis.

Sales of medical equipment: Some businesses generate additional revenue by selling medical equipment, such as oxygen tanks or defibrillators, to their clients.

Here are a few actionable tips for starting a Private Ambulance Services Business in Africa:

Obtain the necessary licenses and certifications: To operate a Private Ambulance Services Business, you'll need to obtain the necessary licenses and certifications required by your local government. This might include a business license, ambulance operator's license, and medical certifications for your staff.

Invest in high-quality vehicles: To provide reliable and safe transportation services, it's important to invest in high-quality ambulance vehicles. Consider purchasing new or used vehicles that are equipped with the necessary medical equipment and features.

Hire experienced and qualified staff: To provide high-quality medical care, it's important to hire experienced and qualified staff, including paramedics, EMTs, and drivers. Consider offering ongoing training and development opportunities to keep your staff up-to-date on the latest medical techniques and protocols.

Build a strong marketing and sales strategy: To attract clients, you'll need to have a strong marketing and sales strategy in place. This might involve building a website, creating social media accounts, running online advertising campaigns or networking with potential clients and partners.

Offer a range of services: To appeal to a wide range of clients, it can be helpful to offer a range of services beyond just transport. This might include medical equipment sales, contract work with healthcare providers, or specialized medical transportation services, such as air ambulance services.

Overall, a Private Ambulance Services Business can be a lucrative and rewarding venture in Africa, provided that you are able to obtain the necessary licenses (maybe approval from ministry of health depending your location), invest in high-quality vehicles, hire experienced and qualified staff, build a strong marketing and sales strategy, and offer a range of services. With the right approach and hard work, you can build a successful and sustainable business in this important and growing industry.

CHAPTER 31:

CIVIL ENGINEERING FIRM
BUSINESS MODEL

A Civil Engineering Firm Business is a company that provides engineering services related to the design, construction, and maintenance of infrastructure projects, such as buildings, water and sewage systems to an extent roads and bridges. The business model for a Civil Engineering Firm in Africa is fairly straightforward: the firm provides engineering services to clients in exchange for a fee.

There are several ways that a Civil Engineering Firm Business can make money in Africa:

Engineering services: The primary way that a Civil Engineering Firm makes money is by providing engineering services to clients. These services might include design, construction

213

management, project management, and maintenance services.

Consulting fees: Some firms also offer consulting services, which can generate additional revenue. This might involve providing advice on infrastructure projects, conducting feasibility studies, or developing plans and specifications.

Sales of equipment and materials: Some firms generate revenue by selling equipment and materials to clients, such as construction materials, tools, and software.

Research and development: Some firms conduct research and development in civil engineering technologies and methods, and may generate revenue by licensing their intellectual property to other companies or through grants or funding from government agencies or other organizations.

Here are a few actionable tips for starting a Civil Engineering Firm Business in Africa:

Build your expertise: To be successful in this field, it's important to have a deep understanding of civil engineering principles and to be able to effectively communicate this knowledge to clients. Consider obtaining relevant certifications, such as a Professional Engineer (PE) license, or pursuing additional education.

Develop a strong business plan: A well-thought-out business plan will help you to identify your target market, define your services, and set goals for your company. It will also be useful when seeking funding or investors.

Build a network of contacts: As a civil engineering firm, you will need to work with a variety of professionals, including architects, contractors, and government officials. Building a strong network of contacts in the industry can help you to find new clients and projects.

Obtain the necessary licenses and certifications: In order to operate legally, you will need to obtain the necessary licenses and certifications for your business. This may include a business license, engineering licenses, and any other certifications required by local laws.

Market your business: Once you have your business plan in place and the necessary licenses and certifications, it's time to start marketing your firm. This may include creating a website, networking with potential clients, and advertising your services through social media and other channels.

Build a strong team: As your business grows, you will need to hire employees to help you manage projects and serve your clients. It's important to build a strong team of professionals who are skilled and dedicated to delivering high-quality work.

Stay up-to-date with industry trends and developments: The field of civil engineering is constantly evolving, and it's important to stay up-to-date with the latest trends and developments. This may include taking continuing education courses, attending industry conferences, and reading industry publications.

CHAPTER 32:

LEGAL AID SERVICES AGENCY BUSINESS MODEL

A Legal Aid Services Agency Business Model is a business that provides legal assistance and representation to individuals and organizations who are unable to afford it.

In Africa, this type of business can make money in several ways:

<u>Charging clients for services:</u> This is the most common way for legal aid agencies to make money. Clients may be charged a flat fee or an hourly rate for the services they receive.

<u>Grant funding:</u> Many legal aid agencies in Africa receive funding from government or non-profit organizations in the form of grants. These grants

218

can help cover the cost of providing legal services to those in need.

Private donations: Some legal aid agencies may also rely on private donations from individuals or organizations to fund their operations.

Pro bono work: Some legal aid agencies may also engage in pro bono work, which is the practice of providing legal services for free or at a reduced rate to those in need.

Actionable tips for young entrepreneurs looking to start a Legal Aid Services Agency in Africa:

- Research the legal aid market in your area to determine the demand for such services and how you can differentiate your business from competitors.

- Network with local lawyers and legal professionals to build relationships and establish yourself as a trusted provider of legal services.

- Consider seeking grant funding or private donations to help fund your business, as well as engaging in pro bono work to help those in need.

- Invest in marketing and outreach efforts to reach potential clients and make them aware of your services.

In summary, a Legal Aid Services Agency Business Model in Africa can make money by charging clients for services, seeking grant funding, accepting private donations, and engaging in pro bono work. By conducting market research, networking with legal professionals, seeking funding, and marketing your services, you can establish your business as a trusted provider of legal assistance to those in need.

Legal aid agencies typically provide a wide range of services to individuals and institutions, including:

Legal representation in court: Legal aid agencies may provide representation in court for individuals and organizations who are unable to afford a private attorney.

Legal advice and counseling: Many legal aid agencies offer advice and counseling to individuals and organizations on a variety of legal issues, such as child custody, divorce, bankruptcy, and employment law.

Legal document preparation: Some legal aid agencies may also provide assistance with preparing legal documents, such as wills, contracts, and power of attorney documents.

<u>Mediation and dispute resolution:</u> Some legal aid agencies may offer mediation and dispute resolution services to help parties resolve conflicts and reach agreements outside of court.

<u>Community education and outreach:</u> Legal aid agencies may also engage in community education and outreach efforts to raise awareness about legal issues and the services they offer.

<u>Advocacy and policy work:</u> Some legal aid agencies may also engage in advocacy and policy work to promote changes in laws and policies that benefit disadvantaged or marginalized groups.

CHAPTER 33:

BUYING AND SELLING OF LANDS BUSINESS MODEL

A Buying and Selling of Lands Business Model is a business that buys and sells land for a profit.

In Africa, this type of business can make money in several ways:

Buying land at a low price: The business can buy land at a low price from sellers who are motivated to sell quickly or who are unable to hold onto the land for financial reasons. The business can then sell the land for a higher price, resulting in a profit.

Developing land and selling it: The business can purchase land, develop it with infrastructure such as roads and buildings, and then sell it at a higher price.

Renting out land: The business can purchase land and then rent it out to individuals or organizations for a regular income.

Providing land management services: The business can also offer land management services, such as overseeing the maintenance and development of land for clients.

Actionable tips for young entrepreneurs looking to start a Buying and Selling of Lands Business in Africa:

- Research the real estate market in your area to understand the demand for land and the going rates for buying and selling.

- Network with real estate professionals and investors to find potential deals and build relationships.

- Consider offering a range of services, such as land development, management, and rental, to diversify your revenue streams.

- Invest in marketing and outreach efforts to reach potential buyers and sellers and make them aware of your services.

In summary, a Buying and Selling of Lands Business Model in Africa can make money by buying land at a low price and selling it for a profit, developing land and selling it, renting out land, and providing land management services. By conducting market research, networking with industry professionals, offering a range of services, and marketing your business, you can establish yourself as a trusted provider of land buying and selling services in Africa.

CHAPTER 34:

REAL ESTATE FIRM BUSINESS MODEL

A Real Estate Firm Business Model is a business that buys, sells, and manages real estate properties such as homes, office buildings, and land.

In Africa, this type of business can make money in several ways:

Buying and selling properties: Real estate firms can make money by buying properties at a low price and then selling them at a higher price, resulting in a profit.

Renting out properties: Real estate firms can also make money by purchasing properties and then renting them out to individuals or organizations for a regular income.

226

Managing properties for clients: Real estate firms can also offer property management services to clients, such as overseeing the maintenance and development of properties, and charging a fee for these services.

Providing real estate brokerage services: Real estate firms may also act as brokers, connecting buyers and sellers of properties and charging a commission for their services.

Actionable tips for young entrepreneurs looking to start a Real Estate Firm in Africa:

- Research the real estate market in your area to understand the demand for different types of properties and the going rates for buying and selling.

- Network with real estate professionals, investors, and potential clients to build relationships and establish yourself as a trusted provider of real estate services.

- Consider offering a range of services, such as property sales, rentals, management, and brokerage, to diversify your revenue streams.

- Invest in marketing and outreach efforts to reach potential buyers and sellers and make them aware of your services.

- Secure the necessary licenses and permits to operate your business legally.

- Build a professional website and use social media and other online platforms to market your business and reach potential clients.

- Consider partnering with other businesses or professionals to expand your reach and offer additional services to clients.

- Keep up to date with industry trends and developments, and continuously work to improve and expand your business.

In summary, a Real Estate Firm Business Model in Africa can make money by buying and selling properties, renting out properties, managing properties for clients, and providing brokerage services. By conducting market research, networking with industry professionals, offering a range of services, and marketing your business, you can establish yourself as a trusted provider of real estate services in Africa.

CHAPTER 35:

EXCLUSIVE PRODUCT DISTRIBUTION BUSINESS MODEL

An Exclusive Product Distribution Business is a business that has the exclusive rights to distribute a particular product or product line within a specific geographic region at wholesale level. The entrepreneur can approach a manufacturer to a sign an exlusive deal.

Selling products to retailers: The business can make money by selling the products it distributes to retailers, such as supermarkets and stores, at a wholesale price.

Selling products directly to consumers: The business can also sell the products it distributes directly to consumers through its own retail outlets or online.

Charging fees for distribution services: The business can also charge fees to manufacturers or other companies for the distribution services it provides.

Providing additional services: The business can also offer additional services to manufacturers or retailers, such as marketing and advertising support, and charge fees for these services.

Actionable tips for young entrepreneurs looking to start an Exclusive Product Distribution Business in Africa:

- Research the market and identify a product or product line that has a high demand and is not widely available in your region.

- Negotiate exclusive distribution rights with the manufacturer or supplier of the product.

231

- Build relationships with retailers and other potential clients to establish yourself as a trusted provider of distribution services.

- Consider offering additional services, such as marketing and advertising support, to manufacturers and retailers to diversify your revenue streams.

- Invest in marketing and outreach efforts to promote the products you distribute and make them more widely available to consumers.

In summary, an Exclusive Product Distribution Business in Africa can make money by selling products to retailers, selling products directly to consumers, charging fees for distribution services, and providing additional services to manufacturers and retailers. By conducting market rescarch, negotiating distribution rights, building relationships with clients, offering additional services, and promoting the products you distribute, you can establish yourself as a trusted provider of distribution services in Africa.

CHAPTER 36:

BUSINESS INCUBATION FIRM
BUSINESS MODEL

A Business Incubation Firm Business is a business that provides support and resources to help early-stage companies and entrepreneurs develop and grow their businesses.

In Africa, this type of business can make money in several ways:

<u>Charging fees for incubation services:</u> The business can charge fees to the companies and entrepreneurs it supports for the incubation services it provides, such as office space, mentorship, and access to resources.

<u>Investing in incubated companies:</u> The business can also invest in the companies it supports and

receive a return on investment when the companies are successful.

Providing additional services: The business can also offer additional services to incubated companies and entrepreneurs, such as marketing and advertising support, and charge fees for these services.

Receiving funding from external sources: The business can also receive funding from external sources, such as government agencies or non-profit organizations, to support its operations and the companies it incubates.

Actionable tips for young entrepreneurs looking to start a Business Incubation Firm in Africa:

- Research the business incubation market in your area to understand the demand for incubation services and how you can differentiate your business from competitors.

- Build relationships with potential clients and partners, such as early-stage companies and entrepreneurs, to establish yourself as a trusted provider of incubation services.

- Consider offering a range of services, such as office space, mentorship, access to resources, and marketing and advertising support, to incubated companies and entrepreneurs.

- Seek funding from external sources, such as government agencies or non-profit organizations, to support your business and the companies you incubate.

- Invest in marketing and outreach efforts to reach potential clients and partners and make them aware of your services.

In summary, a Business Incubation Firm Business in Africa can make money by charging fees for incubation services, investing in incubated companies, providing additional services, and receiving funding from external sources. By conducting market research, building relationships with potential clients and partners, offering a range of services, and seeking funding, you can establish yourself as a trusted provider of incubation services in Africa.

CHAPTER 37:

CO-WORKING SPACE BUSINESS MODEL

A Co-Working Space Business is a business that provides a shared workspace environment for individuals and organizations to work, collaborate, and network.

In Africa, this type of business can make money in several ways:

<u>Charging membership fees:</u> The business can charge individuals and organizations a monthly or annual membership fee to use the co-working space.

<u>Renting out private office space:</u> The business can also rent out private office space to individuals or organizations on a monthly or yearly basis.

Providing additional services: The business can also offer additional services, such as meeting room rentals, printing and copying services, and networking events, and charge fees for these services.

Renting out event space: The business can also rent out event space for meetings, conferences, and other events, and charge a fee for the use of the space.

Actionable tips for young entrepreneurs looking to start a Co-Working Space Business in Africa:

- Research the co-working market in your area to understand the demand for shared workspace and how you can differentiate your business from competitors.

- Consider offering a range of membership options, such as daily, monthly, and annual memberships, to appeal to a wider range of clients.

- Invest in marketing and outreach efforts to reach potential members and make them aware of your services.

- Offer additional services, such as meeting room rentals and networking events, to provide value to members and generate additional revenue.

- Consider partnering with other businesses or organizations to offer additional services or to expand your reach.

In summary, a Co-Working Space Business in Africa can make money by charging membership fees, renting out private office space, providing additional services, and renting out event space. By conducting market research, offering a range of membership options, marketing your services, and offering additional services, you can establish yourself as a trusted provider of co-working space in Africa.

CHAPTER 38:

COFFEE SHOP & CO-WORKING SPACE BUSINESS MODEL

A Coffee Shop & Co-Working Space is a business that combines a traditional coffee shop with a shared workspace environment.

In Africa, this type of business can make money in several ways:

<u>Selling coffee and food:</u> The business can make money by selling coffee, tea, and other beverages, as well as food items such as sandwiches and pastries.

<u>Charging membership fees:</u> The business can charge individuals and organizations a monthly or annual membership fee to use the co-working space.

242

<u>Renting out private meeting rooms</u>: The business can also rent out private meeting rooms to individuals or organizations on an hourly or daily basis.

<u>Providing additional services</u>: The business can also offer additional services, such as printing and copying services, and charge fees for these services.

<u>Hosting events</u>: The business can also host events, such as workshops, lectures, and networking events, and charge a fee for the use of the space.

Actionable tips for young entrepreneurs looking to start a Coffee Shop & Co-Working Space in Africa:

- Research the coffee and co-working markets in your area to understand the demand for these services and how you can differentiate your business from competitors.

- Offer a range of membership options, such as daily, monthly, and annual memberships, to appeal to a wider range of clients.

- Invest in marketing and outreach efforts to reach potential customers and members and make them aware of your services.

- Offer additional services, such as meeting room rentals and printing and copying services, to provide value to customers and members and generate additional revenue.

- Consider hosting events, such as workshops and networking events, to attract new customers and members and provide additional revenue streams.

In summary, a Coffee Shop & Co-Working Space in Africa can make money by selling coffee and food, charging membership fees, renting out private meeting rooms, providing additional services, and hosting events. By conducting market research,

244

offering a range of membership options, marketing your services, and offering additional services, you can establish yourself as a trusted provider of coffee and co-working services in Africa

CHAPTER 39:

MENTAL HEALTH & DEPRESSION COUNSELLING AGENCY BUSINESS MODEL

A Mental Health & Depression Counselling Agency Business is a business that provides mental health and depression counselling services to individuals and organizations. In Africa, this type of business can make money in several ways:

Charging fees for counselling services: The business can charge individuals and organizations a fee for the counselling services it provides.

Partnering with insurance companies: The business can also partner with insurance companies to provide counselling services to policyholders and receive reimbursement for these services.

246

Providing additional services: The business can also offer additional services, such as workshops and seminars, and charge fees for these services.

Receiving funding from external sources: The business can also receive funding from external sources, such as government agencies or non-profit organizations, to support its operations and the services it provides.

Actionable tips for young entrepreneurs looking to start a Mental Health & Depression Counseling Agency Business in Africa:

- Research the mental health and depression counseling market in your area to understand the demand for these services and how you can differentiate your business from competitors.

- Build relationships with potential clients, such as individuals and organizations, to establish yourself as a trusted provider of counseling services.

- Consider partnering with insurance companies to provide counseling services to policyholders and receive reimbursement for these services.

- Offer additional services, such as workshops and seminars, to provide value to clients and generate additional revenue.

CHAPTER 40:

RELATIONSHIP & MARRIAGE COUNSELLING AGENCY BUSINESS MODEL

A Relationship & Marriage Counselling Agency Business is a business that provides relationship and marriage counselling services to individuals and couples.

In Africa, this type of business can make money in several ways:

Charging fees for counselling services: The business can charge individuals and couples a fee for the counselling services it provides.

Partnering with insurance companies: The business can also partner with insurance companies to provide counselling services to policyholders and receive reimbursement for these services.

Providing additional services: The business can also offer additional services, such as workshops and seminars, and charge fees for these services.

Receiving funding from external sources: The business can also receive funding from external sources, such as government agencies or non-profit organizations, to support its operations and the services it provides.

Actionable tips for young entrepreneurs looking to start a Relationship & Marriage Counselling Agency Business in Africa:

- Research the relationship and marriage counselling market in your area to understand the demand for these services and how you can differentiate your business from competitors.

- Build relationships with potential clients, such as individuals and couples, to establish yourself as a trusted provider of counselling services.

- Consider partnering with insurance companies to provide counselling services to policyholders and receive reimbursement for these services.

- Offer additional services, such as workshops and seminars, to provide value to clients and generate additional revenue.

- Invest in marketing and outreach efforts to reach potential clients and make them aware of your services.

In summary, a Relationship & Marriage Counseling Agency Business in Africa can make money by charging fees for counseling services, partnering with insurance companies, providing additional services, and receiving funding from external sources. By conducting market research, building relationships with potential clients, offering additional services, and marketing your business, you can establish yourself as a trusted provider of relationship and marriage counseling services in Africa.

A Relationship & Marriage Counseling Agency can provide a range of services to individuals and couples, including:

Individual and couples therapy sessions: These sessions provide a safe and confidential space for individuals and couples to explore and address issues in their relationships, such as communication problems, trust issues, and conflict resolution.

Marriage preparation and enrichment counseling: These services can help couples prepare for marriage or improve and strengthen their existing relationships.

Family therapy: These sessions can help families address and resolve conflicts, improve communication and relationship dynamics, and support family members in coping with life challenges.

Workshops and seminars: The agency can also offer workshops and seminars on topics such as communication skills, conflict resolution, and building healthy relationships.

Online counselling: Some agencies may also offer counselling services online through video or phone calls to make it more convenient for clients to access support.

Pre-marital counselling: This type of counselling helps couples prepare for marriage by discussing and addressing potential challenges and issues that may arise in the relationship.

Relationship coaching: This service provides guidance and support to individuals and couples who want to improve their relationships and communication skills.

Group therapy: This type of therapy brings together a group of individuals or couples with similar issues or challenges to discuss and explore solutions together in a supportive and confidential environment.

Parenting support and guidance: The agency can also offer support and guidance to parents on topics such as parenting styles, discipline, and managing family dynamics.

Infidelity counseling: This type of counseling can help couples heal and rebuild trust after an affair has occurred.

By Dr. Javnyuy Joybert

CHAPTER 41:

BUSINESS FINANCING AGENCY

BUSINESS MODEL

A Business Financing Agency is a company that provides financial assistance to small and medium-sized businesses in the form of loans, grants, and other forms of financing. These agencies typically work with banks and other financial institutions to provide businesses with the capital they need to start or expand their operations.

There are several ways that a Business Financing Agency can make money in Africa:

Interest on loans: The agency can make money by charging interest on the loans it provides to businesses. This is a common way for lending institutions to generate revenue.

Service fees: The agency may charge a fee for its services, such as for loan processing or for providing financial consulting services.

Commission: The agency may receive a commission from banks and other financial institutions for referring businesses to them for financing.

Equity investment: In some cases, the agency may take an equity stake in the businesses it finances in exchange for capital.

Government grants: Some Business Financing Agencies may receive funding from government grants or other sources of public funding.

Here are some actionable tips for young entrepreneurs looking to work with a Business Financing Agency:

Research different agencies: It's important to do your homework and compare different Business Financing Agencies to find the one that best fits your needs. Look for agencies that have a good track record and a reputation for working with small businesses.

Understand the terms of the financing: Make sure you understand the terms of the financing, including the interest rate, repayment period, and any fees or charges that may apply.

Have a solid business plan: A strong business plan is crucial for securing financing from a Business Financing Agency. Make sure to include detailed financial projections and a clear description of your business concept and target market.

In conclusion, a Business Financing Agency is a valuable resource for small and medium-sized businesses in Africa looking for financial assistance.

By understanding the different ways these agencies make money and taking the time to research and prepare a solid business plan, young entrepreneurs can increase their chances of securing the financing they need to grow their businesses.

There are many services and products that a business financing agency can provide to individuals and businesses in Africa. Some examples include:

<u>**Business loans:**</u> Financing agencies can provide loans to businesses in Africa to help them start or expand their operations.

<u>**Microfinance:**</u> These agencies can offer small loans to individuals and microenterprises in Africa who may not qualify for traditional bank loans.

<u>**Leasing:**</u> Financing agencies can provide equipment leasing services to businesses in Africa,

which allows them to acquire the equipment they need without having to pay the full upfront cost.

Invoice financing: This service allows businesses in Africa to receive financing based on the value of their outstanding invoices.

Trade finance: Financing agencies can provide trade finance services, such as letters of credit and other financial instruments, to businesses in Africa to support their import and export activities.

Agricultural financing: These agencies can provide financing to farmers and other agricultural businesses in Africa to help them grow and sustain their operations.

Real estate financing: Financing agencies can provide financing to individuals and businesses in Africa who are looking to purchase or renovate commercial or residential properties.

Energy financing: These agencies can provide financing to businesses in Africa that are looking to invest in renewable energy projects or upgrade their energy infrastructure.

CHAPTER 42:

AGRIBUSINESS MARKETING FIRM BUSINESS MODEL

An agribusiness marketing firm is a business that helps agriculture-based companies in Africa market their products and services to a wider audience. Agribusiness marketing firms can provide a range of services, including market research, branding and packaging design, advertising, and sales support.

There are several ways that agribusiness marketing firms can make money in Africa:

Service fees: Agribusiness marketing firms can charge a fee for the marketing services they provide to their clients.

Commission-based sales: Some agribusiness marketing firms may earn a commission on sales made as a result of their marketing efforts.

Advertising revenue: Agribusiness marketing firms may also generate revenue by selling advertising space on their website or other marketing materials.

Product sales: Some agribusiness marketing firms may also sell their own products, such as marketing software or training courses, to their clients.

To succeed as an agribusiness marketing firm in Africa, it is important to have a deep understanding of the agriculture industry and the specific needs of your clients. You should also have a strong network of contacts and be able to build relationships with key decision-makers in the industry. Finally, you should be able to effectively communicate the value of your marketing services to potential clients and demonstrate the results you can deliver.

In summary, agribusiness marketing firms in Africa can make money by charging fees for their marketing services, earning commissions on sales, generating advertising revenue, and selling their own products. By building strong relationships, understanding the needs of their clients, and effectively communicating the value of their services, agribusiness marketing firms can thrive in the African market.

Here are some practical, actionable tips for starting an agribusiness marketing firm in Africa:

Conduct market research: It is important to thoroughly research the agriculture industry in Africa to understand the needs of your potential clients and the competition you will face.

Identify your target market: Determine which types of agriculture-based businesses you want to work with and focus on building relationships with those companies.

Develop a strong value proposition: Clearly communicate the value of your marketing services and how you can help your clients grow their businesses.

Build a network: Networking is key in the agribusiness industry. Attend industry events, join professional associations, and build relationships with key decision-makers in the industry.

Establish a strong online presence: In today's digital age, it is important to have a strong online presence. Create a professional website, maintain an active social media presence, and consider using digital marketing strategies to reach potential clients.

Offer a range of services: Consider offering a range of marketing services, such as market research, branding and packaging design, advertising, and sales support. This will allow you to meet the diverse needs of your clients.

Stay up to date on industry trends: Keep track of the latest trends and developments in the agriculture industry in Africa to stay ahead of the competition and better serve your clients.

Build a strong team: As your business grows, consider hiring a team of marketing professionals who can bring a range of skills and expertise to your firm.

By following these tips, you can successfully start and grow an agribusiness marketing firm in Africa.

CHAPTER 43:

DAY-CARE BUSINESS MODEL

A day-care business is a type of business that provides care for children during the day, typically while their parents are at work or busy with other responsibilities. In Africa, day-care businesses can be found in both urban and rural areas, and they may be run by individuals, families, or larger organizations.

There are several ways that a day-care business can make money in Africa. One common method is by charging fees to parents for the care and supervision of their children. These fees may be based on a variety of factors, such as the age of the child, the length of time they will be in the day-care, and the specific services being provided.

Another way that a day-care business can make money is by offering additional services or programs, such as early childhood education, after-school care, or summer camps. These services may be offered for an additional fee or as part of a package deal.

Finally, day-care businesses may also generate income through partnerships or sponsorships with local businesses or organizations. For example, a day-care business may work with a local school to provide after-school care for students, or they may partner with a local business to offer on-site childcare for employees.

Some actionable tips for starting a day-care business in Africa include:

- Research the local market to determine the demand for day-care services in your area.

- Develop a clear business plan that outlines your target market, services offered, and pricing structure.

- Obtain any necessary licenses or certifications to operate a day-care in your area.

- Build relationships with local businesses and organizations to generate additional income streams.

- Invest in quality resources and materials to create a safe and engaging environment for children.

In summary, a day-care business in Africa can make money through fees charged to parents, additional services or programs, and partnerships or sponsorships with local businesses. By carefully planning and executing a solid business model, young entrepreneurs can successfully start and operate a successful day-care business in Africa.

Day-care businesses typically provide a range of services to parents, including:

Childcare: The primary function of a day-care is to provide care and supervision for children during the day. This may include activities such as playtime, naptime, and mealtime.

Early childhood education: Many day-care businesses also offer early childhood education programs to help children learn and develop important skills. These programs may include activities such as reading, writing, and math lessons, as well as hands-on projects and activities.

Before and after school care: Some day-care businesses offer care for children before and after school hours, allowing parents to drop off and pick up their children at the day-care rather than at school.

Summer camps: Many day-care businesses also offer summer camps or other vacation programs to provide care and entertainment for children during school breaks.

Special needs support: Some day-care businesses may have specialized staff or programs to support children with special needs or disabilities.

Health and safety: Day-care businesses are responsible for maintaining a safe and healthy environment for children, which may include providing meals, snacks, and drinks, as well as maintaining clean and sanitary facilities.

Parent communication: Many day-care businesses also provide regular updates and communication to parents about their child's development and activities at the day-care.

By Dr. Javnyuy Joybert

CHAPTER 44:

SNACK HOME MAKING &

DELIVERY BUSINESS MODEL

A snack home making and delivery business is a type of food business that specializes in the production and delivery of snacks, such as cookies, cakes, pastries, and other baked goods. This type of business may operate out of a brick and mortar storefront, a food truck, or a home kitchen, and may deliver products directly to customers or sell them through other channels, such as online or at local markets or events.

There are several ways that a snack home making and delivery business can make money in Africa. One common method is through the sale of snacks directly to customers, either through online orders, walk-in sales at a storefront, or at local markets or events. This business model relies on the demand

273

for high-quality, convenient snack options in the local market.

Another way that a snack home making and delivery business can make money is through partnerships or wholesale agreements with local businesses or organizations. For example, a snack business may sell its products to local coffee shops, restaurants, or other food-related businesses, or it may partner with event planners or caterers to provide snacks for events and gatherings.

Some actionable tips for starting a snack home making and delivery business in Africa include:

- Research the local market to determine the demand for snack options and the competition in your area.

- Develop a clear business plan that outlines your target market, product offerings, and pricing structure.

- Obtain any necessary licenses or certifications to operate a food business in your area (if necessary).

- Invest in quality ingredients and equipment to ensure the production of high-quality snacks.

- Build relationships with local businesses and organizations to generate additional income streams through partnerships and wholesale agreements.

In summary, a snack home making and delivery business in Africa can make money through the direct sale of snacks to customers, as well as through partnerships and wholesale agreements with local businesses. By carefully planning and executing a solid business model, young entrepreneurs can successfully start and operate a successful snack home making and delivery business in Africa.

By Dr. Javnyuy Joybert